Better Homes and Gardens.

MEATLESS
MAIN DISHES

© 1981 by Meredith Corporation, Des Moines, Iowa.
All Rights Reserved. Printed in the United States of America.
First Edition. First Printing.
Library of Congress Catalog Card Number: 80-68539
ISBN: 0-696-00645-6

On the cover: *Spicy Paella-Style Vegetables,* a meatless version of the classic Spanish paella, features sunny poached eggs nestled on a bed of peppery rice (see recipe, page 66).

Meatless Main Dishes
Editors: Julia Martinusen, Marcia Stanley, Pat Teberg
Copy and Production Editor: David Kirchner
Graphic Designer: Faith Berven

BETTER HOMES AND GARDENS® BOOKS
Editor: Gerald M. Knox
Art Director: Ernest Shelton

Food and Nutrition Editor: Doris Eby
Senior Food Editor: Sharyl Heiken
Senior Associate Food Editors: Sandra Granseth, Elizabeth Woolever
Associate Food Editors: Bonnie Lasater, Julia Martinusen, Marcia Stanley, Joy Taylor, Pat Teberg, Diana Tryon
Recipe Development Editor: Marion Viall
Test Kitchen Director: Sharon Golbert
Test Kitchen Home Economists: Jean Brekke, Kay Cargill, Marilyn Cornelius, Maryellyn Krantz, Marge Steenson

Copy and Production Editors: David Kirchner, Lamont Olson, David A. Walsh

Associate Art Directors: Neoma Alt West, Randall Yontz
Assistant Art Director: Harijs Priekulis
Senior Graphic Designer: Faith Berven
Graphic Designers: Alisann Dixon, Linda Ford, Lynda Haupert, Tom Wegner

Editor-in-Chief: James A. Autry
Editorial Director: Neil Kuehnl
Group Administrative Editor: Duane Gregg
Executive Art Director: William J. Yates

Our seal assures you that every recipe in *Meatless Main Dishes* is endorsed by the Better Homes and Gardens Test Kitchen. Each recipe is tested for family appeal, practicality, and deliciousness.

CONTENTS

MAKE IT MEATLESS

Though they're often economical and definitely delicious, meatless meals require a bit of extra planning to be nutritionally complete. This chapter explains how to plan meatless meals and balance protein for healthy eating. Read it first and start your meatless adventure on a sound nutritional footing.

The Basic Five Food Groups

MAKE·IT·MEATLESS

Why make it meatless? Because meatless eating offers you an alternate form of protein that is often quite economical. But in addition, main dishes without meat let you experience a variety of enticing textures and flavors. In Meatless Main Dishes, you'll not only find recipes that look as delicious as they taste (for proof, just turn to page 40 or 43), but that also meet the trusted quality and nutrition standards of Better Homes and Gardens.

Meatless cooking encompasses everything from the familiar to the exotic—from our Cashew-Sprout Omelet to our crunchy Vegetable-Nut Loaf topped with sour cream. And because we wanted the entrées to be outstanding, we've called for some ingredients—Brie cheese or fettucini, for example—that you might not use regularly. You won't need to go to a health food store to buy them, but to help you find them in your supermarket or to explain how they taste, we've included identification charts for cheese, pasta, legumes, salad greens, and unusual vegetables.

Planning a meatless meal involves a lot more than just omitting the hamburger from the chili. As you read through the next few pages, you'll see what's involved in substituting other forms of protein for meat to create nutritionally sound meals. Then to help you plan side dishes, desserts, and beverages to serve with your meatless main dishes, we've included an entire chapter of menus. It not only aids you in planning meatless meals but it also shows how accompanying foods help to meet your protein needs.

Try a meatless meal. You'll be pleasantly surprised at the variety it will bring to your table.

THE BASIC FIVE FOOD GROUPS

It's a basic nutrition principle that no one food is "perfect" by itself. That's why it's important to eat a variety of foods for a good nutrition balance. It sounds complicated but it's not. The Basic Five Food Groups were developed as a guide to help you plan a nutritionally sound diet. Until recently, there were only four basic food groups. But because some foods provide little or no nutritional value in relation to the calories they contain, these foods were dropped from the basic four. Now they comprise a fifth group—the Fats, Sweets, and Alcohol Food Group. So now there are Five Basic Food Groups, including the Dairy Food Group, the Protein-Rich Food Group, the Breads and Cereals Food Group, the Fruits and Vegetables Food Group, and the Fats, Sweets, and Alcohol Food Group. Choosing a variety of foods from the following Basic Five guidelines ensures that you're getting nutrients for growth and maintenance.

6

The **Dairy Food Group** contributes calcium, riboflavin, protein, vitamin A, and vitamin D to your diet. Adults need 2 servings daily, children under nine need 2 to 3 servings daily, children over nine need 3 servings daily, and teenagers need 4 servings daily. One serving from this group of foods is the equivalent of 1 cup milk. Or, you can substitute 1 cup yogurt, 1½ cups ice cream, 2 ounces cheese, 2 cups cottage cheese, 1 cup buttermilk, 1 cup skim milk, or 1 cup low-fat milk.

Beef, veal, lamb, pork, poultry, fish, shellfish, dry beans, dry peas, soybeans, lentils, eggs, seeds, nuts, and peanut butter are all included in the **Protein-Rich Food Group**, from which you need 2 servings daily. Count 2 to 3 ounces of cooked meat, poultry, or fish as a serving. Two eggs, 1 to 1½ cups cooked dry beans, dry peas, soybeans, or lentils, ¼ cup peanut butter, or ½ to 1 cup nuts, sesame seed, or sunflower seed also count as one serving of protein-rich foods. This group of foods provides you not only with protein, but also with phosphorus, iron, thiamine,

niacin, and riboflavin. When planning daily menus, it's a good idea to vary your selections from these foods because each has its own nutritional advantages (see Substituting Protein, page 11).

Cereals, breads, crackers, pasta, rice, and grits are just some of the foods included in the **Breads and Cereals Food Group**, which provides B vitamins, iron, and protein. Often you'll find that cereals and breads have been enriched. This means that nutrients have been added —more than were in the original ingredients. In fact, some contain vitamins such as A, B, C, and D that are not normally found in these foods. However, since all refined products (enriched or not) may be low in other vitamins and trace minerals, you should include some whole-grain products in your diet.

One serving from the Breads and Cereals Food Group is equal to one slice of bread, one ounce of ready-to-eat cereal, or ½ cup of cooked cereal, rice, pasta, or grits. You need at least four servings daily from this wide range of foods.

7

You also need four servings daily from the **Fruits and Vegetables Food Group** to ensure that you get adequate amounts of vitamins A and C. A serving is equal to ½ cup fruit or vegetable, or a typical portion, such as 1 orange, half of a grapefruit, or 1 potato. A good source of vitamin A, such as dark-green or deep-yellow vegetables, is needed at least every other day. And a good source of vitamin C, such as citrus fruit or juice, is needed at least once a day. After meeting these requirements, select any other fruits and vegetables to give the menu variety and to add up to the needed four or more servings daily.

The newest addition to the Basic Five Food Groups is the **Fats, Sweets, and Alcohol Food Group.** Foods in this group —such as butter, margarine, mayonnaise, salad dressing, candy, sugar, jelly, soft drinks, alcoholic beverages, and unenriched breads or pastries—provide plenty of calories but few nutrients. That's why there is no suggested number of daily servings for this group. The amount of these foods you should include in your diet depends primarily on how many calories you need after you've met the requirements of the other four food groups.

PROTEIN, FAT, AND CARBOHYDRATES

It's important to use the Basic Five Food Groups to ensure that you get all the nutrients your body needs. Even the lack of one essential nutrient in your diet can cause health problems.

Protein provided by the Protein-Rich, Dairy, Fruits and Vegetables, and Breads and Cereals Food Groups is necessary to build, maintain, and repair the body. It also is involved in the production of healthy red blood cells, antibodies that prevent disease, and hormones that regulate the body. Usually your body's needs for energy are met by your intake of fats and carbohydrates. However, if you have not consumed enough fat or carbohydrate to meet your energy needs, then protein will be used for energy.

One of your body's main sources of energy is carbohydrates, which are found in some foods from all of the Basic Five Food Groups. They exist as natural sugars in fresh fruits, vegetables, and some dairy products, and as pure or refined sugars in products such as honey, corn syrup,

brown sugar, molasses, and granulated sugar. Another form of carbohydrate is starch, which is found in potatoes, beans, breads, cereals, and pasta.

A form of energy more concentrated than carbohydrates is fats. Fats can be obtained from any of the Five Basic Food Groups. Some obvious forms are butter, shortenings, and fat meat, but you also consume fat in baked products, dressings, nuts, avocados, eggs, and even lean meat.

Even though many people consider fat to be a "negative" addition to their diet, a certain amount of fat is necessary to transport vitamins A, D, E, and K into the body, where they can be absorbed. And it also provides some indispensable fatty acids that are necessary to life.

VITAMINS

In addition to protein, carbohydrates, and fats, you need several vitamins in your diet, each of which carries out a specific function. No matter what your body's source of energy, it cannot be released into your body without vitamins. Vitamins also regulate the way your body builds tissue and utilizes food.

Vitamin A, obtained from yellow and leafy green vegetables, cantaloupe, tomatoes, and apricots from the Fruits and Vegetables Food Group and also obtained from foods in the Dairy Food Group, aids in night vision and the prevention of eye disease. It also promotes bone growth and helps to maintain the structure and function of the mucous membranes in the ears, nose, and intestinal lining.

Thiamine (a B vitamin) helps to regulate appetite and maintain a responsive nervous system. It aids in the release of energy from carbohydrates. Include thiamine in your diet by eating enriched breads, cereals, or pasta from the Breads and Cereals Food Group, or pork or nuts from the Protein-Rich Food Group.

9

Riboflavin, another B vitamin, aids in food metabolism, promotes healthy skin, and helps the body use oxygen. It is obtained from foods in the Dairy Food Group, the Protein-Rich Food Group, the Fruits and Vegetables Food Group, and the Breads and Cereals Food Group.

Niacin, the third B vitamin, is obtained from enriched cereals, breads, pasta, or rice in the Breads and Cereals Food Group, from many foods in the Protein-Rich Food Group, and from some foods in the Fruits and Vegetables Food Group. It aids in fat metabolism, tissue respiration, and the conversion of sugar to usable energy.

Vitamin C, also known as ascorbic acid, is plentiful in leafy vegetables, strawberries, citrus fruits, potatoes, tomatoes, and watermelon from the Fruits and Vegetables Food Group. It plays an important part in the formation of collagen, a substance that binds cells together. Vitamin C also is essential for promoting the growth and repair of your bones, teeth, gums, and blood vessels.

MINERALS

Though your body needs only small amounts of minerals, they are nonetheless important. Vitamins would be useless without minerals. And minerals play an important role in blood coagulation.

Calcium, which is contained in foods from the Dairy Food Group and in enriched cereals from the Breads and Cereals Food Group, is needed for growth and maintenance of healthy bones and teeth.

Phosphorus, which promotes firm, supple skin, is found in eggs and tuna from the Protein-Rich Food Group.

Zinc, found in eggs, cheese, meat, poultry, and seafood from the Protein-Rich Food Group and milk from the Dairy Food Group, helps maintain skin elasticity and aids in tissue respiration.

Iron is essential for red blood cells to supply oxygen to the body. It is found in dry beans and meats from the Protein-Rich Food Group, and bran cereals from the Breads and Cereals Food Group.

SUBSTITUTING PROTEIN

One of the main concerns of meatless eating is incorporating enough protein into meals. Although you usually think of meat, fish, or poultry when considering protein, there are many other excellent sources of protein. Eggs, cheese, milk, milk products, nuts, seeds, whole grains, pasta, dry beans, and lentils are just a few of them.

Protein is made up of 22 different components called amino acids. Fourteen of the 22 amino acids can be manufactured in the body. However, the remaining eight amino acids (known as essential amino acids) must be consumed in the food we eat. All eight essential amino acids must be eaten simultaneously for the protein to be properly used.

Animal products make it easy to consume all of the essential amino acids simultaneously because they contain all eight of them. Even though plant products such as nuts, seeds, lentils, dry beans, and whole grains do not provide all of the essential amino acids, it's not hard to plan your diet to include all of them in one meal. Any of the following complementary combinations of food will include all eight essential amino acids: grains and legumes (dry beans, dry peas, or lentils), seeds or nuts and grains, legumes and seeds or nuts, milk products and seeds or nuts, milk products and grains, or milk products and legumes. When these combinations of proteins are eaten together, the protein they provide is utilized by your body just as efficiently as the protein provided by animal products.

When planning a meatless meal, remember that the milk or milk products used to complement amino acids from plant sources are being utilized to meet the requirement for the Protein-Rich Food Group. Be sure to include additional quantities of milk or milk products to meet the Dairy Food Group requirements.

PROTEIN COMPARISONS OF COMMON FOODS

These good sources of protein are listed with the percent U.S. RDA of protein that they provide. U.S. RDA stands for "United States Recommended Daily Allowances," which is a simplified version of the Recommended Dietary Allowances. The RDAs tell the amounts of certain nutrients necessary to meet the nutritional needs of practically all healthy people. You'll also find the percent U.S. RDA of protein per serving provided for all recipes in this book.

Food	Amount	Grams of Protein	U.S. RDA of Protein	Food	Amount	Grams of Protein	U.S. RDA of Protein
Almonds, slivered	½ cup	10.7 grams	16.5%	Macaroni, cooked	1 cup	6.5 grams	10.0%
American cheese	2 ounces	13.2 grams	20.3%	Milk, whole	1 cup	8.5 grams	13.1%
Barley	1 cup	16.4 grams	25.2%	Navy beans	1 cup	14.0 grams	21.5%
Bulgur	1 cup	8.4 grams	12.9%	Parmesan cheese	2 ounces	20.4 grams	31.4%
Brick cheese	2 ounces	12.6 grams	19.4%	Peanut butter	¼ cup	16.2 grams	25.0%
Broccoli	1 cup	4.8 grams	7.4%	Peanuts	½ cup	18.7 grams	28.8%
Cashews, whole	½ cup	12.0 grams	18.5%	Pecans, chopped	½ cup	5.4 grams	8.4%
Cheddar cheese	2 ounces	14.2 grams	21.8%	Pumpkin seeds	¼ cup	10.1 grams	15.6%
Cottage cheese	1 cup	28.6 grams	44.0%	Red kidney beans	1 cup	14.4 grams	22.1%
Cream cheese	2 ounces	4.5 grams	7.0%	Split Peas	1 cup	16.0 grams	24.6%
Eggs	2 eggs	13.0 grams	20.0%	Sunflower seed	¼ cup	8.7 grams	13.4%
Garbanzo beans	1 cup	19.3 grams	29.6%	Swiss cheese	2 ounces	15.6 grams	24.0%
Ground beef	¼ pound	20.3 grams	31.2%	Tofu	¼ pound	8.8 grams	13.6%
Lentils	1 cup	15.6 grams	24.0%	Tuna	¼ pound	32.6 grams	50.2%
Lima beans	1 cup	12.9 grams	19.8%	Walnuts, chopped	½ cup	8.9 grams	13.7%

CHEESE

Asiago

Blue Cheese

Boursin

Brick

Asiago is a hard cheese with a strong, sharp, and slightly salty flavor. It's covered with a smooth, glossy rind, and has small, irregular holes. Asiago is suitable for sandwiches or snacks, but it also can be grated and used the same as grated Parmesan cheese.

Blue cheese is the name used for several varieties of cheeses with distinctive interior vein patterns. Even though they are called blue-veined, the veins actually can be blue, blue-black, or green in color. Blue cheese is strong and pungent in both flavor and aroma and it can be used in salad dressings or with fruit.

Boursin is a buttery-rich, creamy, and tangy cheese that is flavored with pepper, garlic, or herbs. In its natural state, Boursin is pure white, but when flavorings are added, its color depends upon the flavoring. Serve Boursin as an appetizer, on crackers, or on meats.

Brick cheese is often described as a cross between cheddar and Limburger cheese in both texture and flavor. It has a strong, slightly bitter, and tangy flavor, but isn't as strong as Limburger. Its texture is firmer than the Limburger and softer than a cheddar. A brick cheese can be aged for up to three months. The younger the cheese, the milder the flavor and the creamier the texture. Serve brick cheese as an appetizer, with fruit, or on sandwiches.

Brie

Camembert

Cheddar

Cheshire

Brie cheese has a mild aroma and a slightly tangy flavor that complements its smooth and creamy texture. Some Brie is so creamy that it can be spread like a process cheese spread. The interior color varies from cream to golden. A whole Brie cheese is shaped like a disc with a white outer crust. You also can buy portions of Brie cheese either with the crust or in cellophane-wrapped packages.

Camembert is slightly bitter and yeasty in flavor, and is best when eaten at peak ripeness, which is indicated by a white to off-white moldy crust. When the cheese is cut, the soft, almost-fluid consistency of the cheese causes it to bulge out from under its crust. Its creamy texture is slightly sticky, but it can be spread with a knife. Serve Camembert as an appetizer or as a dessert.

Cheddar cheese can be white or orange. The color is often achieved by the addition of dye. It is frequently labeled as being mild, medium, or sharp in flavor, with the longer-aged cheddars more sharp or full-bodied. Cheddar is an all-purpose cheese and can be used in salads, sauces, main dishes, or with many fruits.

Cheshire cheese is a very crumbly, white- to orange-colored cheese with a musty or vinegarish aroma. The flavor is tangy yet mild. Serve it as a snack or in sandwiches.

Colby

Cream Cheese

Edam

Farmer Cheese

Colby cheese is often labeled as being mild or sharp. Mild Colby cheese has a mild, slightly sweet flavor, while the sharp variety is tangy. All Colby cheese has a curdled and rubbery texture similar to cheddar cheese, but with a higher moisture content and a sweeter flavor than cheddar. Serve it as a snack or in sandwiches.

Cream cheese is a rich, fresh cheese. It is soft enough to be spread with a knife. Cream cheese is usually sold as a foil-wrapped block or in a plastic container.

Because it is a fresh cheese, it should be used within a few days of purchase. Cream cheese will add flavor and richness when it is spread on a muffin or bagel, or when it is used in desserts, sauces, casseroles, or fruit toppings.

Edam is a very distinctive-looking cheese—a red paraffin-wax-coated ball with a flattened top and bottom. Beneath the wax is a thin natural rind that covers the light orange, firm-textured cheese. Edam is mild and nutty in flavor. It works well used in appetizers, desserts, main dishes, or sauces.

Several varieties of Edam cheese, such as Baby Edam, Commissie, and Middebare, are also available. These varieties are sized differently than the traditional Edam ball, and sometimes they are flavored with cumin seed, which gives them extra tang.

Feta

Fontina

Gjetost

Gorgonzola

Farmer cheese varies widely in both texture and flavor. Some are dry and crumbly with a slight bitterness or tang, while others are creamy and rubbery with a very mild flavor. Use farmer cheese for salads or with fruit.

Feta is a traditional, soft, white Greek cheese with a sharp and salty flavor. If you find its flavor to be too sharp or salty, soak it in milk to soften the flavor. Its crumbly texture appears wet but feels dry. Serve feta in salads, sandwiches, or casseroles.

Fontina has a rich, distinctive flavor suggestive of cooked milk, with a musty and slightly acidic aftertaste. It is shaped like a flat wheel with a thin, natural rind and some small holes scattered over the smooth, shiny surface. Serve fontina as an appetizer, snack, dessert, or in fondues or casseroles.

Gjetost has a distinctive rich brown color and a hard, solid texture. Its color and flavor are unlike any other cheese. The caramelized flavor is an acquired taste. Serve thinly sliced Gjetost with fruit, or on breads.

Gorgonzola, an off-white cheese with blue veins (they appear to be greenish blue), has a strong, pungent flavor and aroma. It is creamy and salty, but less salty than blue cheese. The longer Gorgonzola is aged, the more robust the flavor. Use Gorgonzola as you would a blue cheese —in salads or with fruit.

13

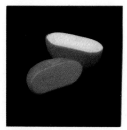

Gouda

Gourmandise

Gruyère

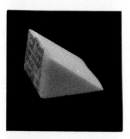

Havarti

Gouda has a yellow-orange interior and is coated with a yellow or red wax. It is shaped like a wheel, with rounded sides and a flat top and bottom. Gouda's flavor is mild and slightly nutty, and its texture is smooth and waxy. Serve Gouda as an appetizer or in salads, sandwiches, snacks, or desserts.

Also available is spiced Gouda, which is a variety that contains cumin seed. It is more firm and tangy than regular Gouda cheese.

Gourmandise is a very rich, smooth, creamy-colored, mild cheese. It is often flavored with garlic, herbs, port wine, cherries, or walnuts. Serve it as a dessert or appetizer.

Gruyère varies from a dry, mealy, strong-flavored, acidic cheese to a creamy, smooth, mild-flavored cheese. Usually the creamier Gruyère is a process cheese, while the drier variety is a natural cheese. Serve Gruyère in appetizers, soups, fondues, or with fruit.

Havarti is a cream-colored cheese that varies in flavor. The younger cheese (aged two to three months) has a mild flavor with a slight aftertaste. Older cheese acquires a pungent flavor.

Havarti has a spongy yellow-to-white texture with small to medium-size irregularly shaped holes scattered throughout the cheese. Serve it as an appetizer, in sandwiches, in snacks, or as a fried cheese. Another variety of Havarti, known

Limburger

Monterey Jack

Mozzarella

Muenster

as Havarti 60, is also available. Havarti 60 has a higher fat content and is richer and creamier than regular Havarti.

Limburger cheese is famous for its very pungent aroma and flavor, and enjoying it is an acquired taste. It has a pale yellow color and a soft and creamy texture. Serve it as a snack or with a strong-flavored vegetable, such as onions, radishes, or shallots.

Monterey Jack cheese has a chewy, almost rubbery consistency and a creamy yellow color. There are two varieties of Monterey Jack—one made from whole milk and the other from skim milk. Both have a mild and nutty flavor with no tang or bitterness. Serve this cheese with fruits or vegetables or as a snack.

Mozzarella cheese has a very mild cheddar taste that is creamy and vaguely sweet. The texture is smooth, plasticlike, and firm. Because of its mild flavor and creamy consistency, it is widely used in cooking.

Muenster cheese varies in texture from moist, porous, and spongy to crumbly and dry, and in flavor from mild to pungent. Muenster cheese made in the United States or Denmark is usually the mild and moist variety, while that made in Germany is the drier, crumbly type. Muenster is usually made in disc shapes and has a thin outer rind. This cheese can be served as a dessert or a snack.

Parmesan

Port du Salut

Provolone

Ricotta

Parmesan is a straw-yellow cheese that tastes slightly nutty and salty. It is a very dry cheese that is made in large cylindrical wheels. However, the grated form is the one most commonly sold. Parmesan cheese will keep almost indefinitely because of its low moisture content. Serve it to complement a great variety of salads, breads, main dishes, or desserts.

Port du Salut cheese is initially mild, buttery, creamy, and smooth, but it develops a delicate, subtle sharpness as an aftertaste. Aged versions of Port du Salut have a more full-bodied and stronger flavor.

It is made in discs about 2 inches high, and has a creamy-yellow interior that is covered by a thin orange rind. Serve it as a snack or dessert.

Provolone cheese varies from mild to sharp, and is smoky flavored. Some people find it salty. It has a cream-colored interior free of holes, and a texture that appears smooth but that feels curdled when eaten. Use it in appetizers, salads, sandwiches, snacks, or as a dessert.

Ricotta is Italian cottage cheese, but it doesn't have curds like the cottage cheese made in the United States. It is white with a very mild flavor and a chalky texture. Ricotta may be dry or wet, depending on the variety.

As with all fresh unripened cheeses, ricotta does not keep for long

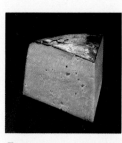

Romano

Roquefort

Sapsago

Swiss

periods of time and should be used soon after purchase. Use it in fillings, spreads, or cheesecakes. When ricotta is cured and salted, it is called dry ricotta and can be grated.

Romano cheese is a dry, hard cheese that is very similar to Parmesan cheese, except that it has a stronger flavor and aroma. Romano can be used on sandwiches or as a snack, or it can be grated and used in the same way as Parmesan.

Roquefort cheese is creamy-white in color, with many blue veins running through it. It has a strong, pungent, salty flavor with a lingering aftertaste. It can be served in the same manner as blue cheese, such as in salads or with fruit.

Sapsago is an unusual cheese. Its light green color comes from the large quantities of dried clover that are added to the curd in the cheese-making process. It has a hard, dry texture and a "grassy" flavor. Sapsago cheese is made in a small cone shape that is no more than 3 inches in diameter at the base and less than 4 inches tall.

Swiss is a very popular cheese with a firm, smooth texture. It has large holes or "eyes" scattered throughout the cheese, and it varies in color from off-white to a rich yellow color. Its sweet and nutty taste makes Swiss excellent as an appetizer, or in casseroles, sandwiches, salads, or snacks.

15

LEGUMES

Garbanzo Beans

Great Northern Beans

Lentils

Navy Beans

Legumes—plants with seed-filled pods, such as beans, lentils, and peas —are an economical source of protein. Cooking dry legumes is easy. For dry black-eyed peas or beans, rinse them and cover with the amount of water specified in the recipe. Let them soak overnight. (Or, if you're in a hurry, skip the overnight soaking and bring the dry beans or black-eyed peas to boiling. Boil 2 minutes and remove from heat. Then soak for 1 hour.) If desired, add ½ teaspoon salt to the soaking water. Bring the beans or black-eyed peas to boiling; reduce the heat and simmer, covered, for 1 hour or till tender. Cooking dry lentils or split peas is even easier. Just rinse them and cover with the amount of water specified in the recipe. Bring to boiling, then reduce the heat and simmer till tender. Allow 35 to 45 minutes for lentils and 1 to 1½ hours for split peas.

Garbanzo beans also are known as chick peas, and are more commonly found canned than dry. They have a slightly nutty flavor and a rough exterior. Use garbanzo beans in appetizers, soups, salads, casseroles, and side dishes.

Great northern beans have a delicate flavor and are commonly found in the dry form. They are large white beans that are used in salads, side dishes, and main dishes.

Lentils are a valuable source of protein in

Pinto Beans

Red Kidney Beans

Soybeans

Split Peas

many areas of the world. They are commonly found dry and have a small, flat, disc shape. Before cooking, most lentils are off-white to green. Their mild flavor makes them ideal for soups and main dishes.

Navy beans also are white beans but are smaller than great northern beans. They are commonly found dry, and their mild flavor also lends them to use in main dishes and soups.

Pinto beans are widely available in the United States either canned or dry. They have a smooth oval shape and are off-white with brown specks. Pinto beans are very versatile and can be used in appetizers, soups, and main dishes.

Red kidney beans are usually found canned or dry. Their name refers to their kidney shape. Red kidney beans are smooth and red in color, and are commonly used in chili.

Soybeans used to be considered only as a field crop and were seldom used for direct human consumption. But their popularity is increasing as more people learn about the many ways they can be served—as a snack, and in appetizers, soups, main dishes, and side dishes.

Split peas are available dry in yellow or green varieties. Sometimes yellow split peas are more difficult to find, but both kinds can be used interchangeably. Use split peas in casseroles, soups, and main dishes.

SOURCES OF PROTEIN

Meat need not be the only source of protein in your diet. Here are some other excellent sources of protein.

Legumes are plants with seed-filled pods, such as beans, lentils, and peas. Although they do not provide all eight essential amino acids, they are a good source of protein when combined with grains, seeds or nuts, or milk products. When you buy dry legumes, inspect the package. Most of the legumes should be whole, with firm, unbroken seed coats. There should be few, if any, holes or cavities, and little discoloration. Dry legumes can be stored in a closed container for a year.

Nuts and seeds are a good source of protein if they are combined with grains or legumes. Store shelled nuts or seeds in a closed container in the refrigerator or freezer. Exclude as much air from the container as possible to keep nuts and seeds from becoming rancid.

Eggs are a good source of protein as well as calcium and iron. Eggs provide all eight essential amino acids, so they needn't be combined with other sources of protein. Eggs can safely be stored in the refrigerator for several weeks, although their quality deteriorates with time.

Yogurt is another complete source of protein as well as a source of calcium and riboflavin. It is made by adding a desirable bacteria to milk. The bacteria converts the milk sugar into lactic acids, which cause the milk to curdle and thicken and produce a tangy flavor. Yogurt may be stored in the refrigerator without any loss of flavor for about 10 days. When yogurt is stored at higher temperatures, a sharp flavor develops, but the yogurt is still edible. If you notice separation of a liquid from the yogurt, stir it back in or pour it off. Fruit-flavored yogurt may be frozen for up to six weeks and then thawed at room temperature for three hours before eating. Plain yogurt is not recommended for freezing.

Cheeses vary widely in texture and flavor (see the identification charts on pages 12 to 15), but all are good sources of protein, calcium, and riboflavin. Hard cheeses such as cheddar, Swiss, and Parmesan may be refrigerated for several weeks, but soft cheeses such as ricotta, Brie, and Camembert are very perishable and should be used within a few days of purchase. Store cheese in the refrigerator in the unopened, original wrapper or tightly covered with foil or clear plastic wrap. Strong-smelling cheeses should be placed in a tightly covered container after wrapping. For longer storage, brick, Camembert, cheddar, Edam, mozzarella, Muenster, Parmesan, Port du Salut, provolone, Romano, and Swiss cheeses may be frozen. To freeze cheese, cut it into chunks no larger than ½ pound and tightly wrap it in a moisture-vapor-proof wrapper. Freeze quickly. Thaw the unopened package in the refrigerator before using.

Of the many forms of protein available, **tofu** is one of the lesser known in the United States. It is a pressed form of soybean curd made from soybean milk that should be used with dairy products, seeds or nuts, or grains. You can purchase tofu as a 12- to 20-ounce water-packed cake in the fresh produce department of many supermarkets, natural food stores, or Oriental food stores. When buying tofu, look for a date stamped on the package. This is the date before which the tofu should be used. The fresher the tofu, the sweeter and lighter the flavor; as tofu ages, it develops a tangy flavor. Use tofu as soon as possible after purchase. If it is necessary to store the tofu for a few days, drain and rinse the tofu, then place it in a container. Cover with fresh water and tightly seal. Drain and change the water daily, then drain the tofu before using it.

MEATLESS MENUS

Take your meatless eating adventure one step further by planning entire meals around your favorite meatless entrées. To whet your appetite (and to show you just how easy it is), we've assembled a chapter full of tempting menus for brunches, lunches, and dinners. Bon appétit!

Vegetable Italian Lasagna, Apple-Almond Salad,
and Peach-Yogurt Pie (See recipes, pages 20 and 21.)

DINNER MENU

Vegetable Italian Lasagna
Apple-Almond Salad
Italian Bread
Peach-Yogurt Pie
Beverage

VEGETABLE ITALIAN LASAGNA

Pictured on pages 18 and 19
Provides 37% U.S. RDA of protein per serving—

- 2 medium carrots, bias sliced
- ⅓ cup chopped onion
- 2 cloves garlic, minced
- 2 tablespoons olive oil *or* cooking oil
- 1 15½-ounce jar extra-thick and zesty meatless spaghetti sauce
- ¼ cup water
- 1½ teaspoons dried oregano, crushed
- ¾ teaspoon salt
- ¾ teaspoon dried basil, crushed
- 1½ cups sliced fresh mushrooms
- 1 small zucchini, cut into bite-size sticks
- 1 10-ounce package frozen chopped spinach, thawed and well drained
- 2 beaten eggs
- 1½ cups cream-style cottage cheese, drained, *or* ricotta cheese
- ¼ cup grated Parmesan cheese
- 6 ounces lasagna noodles, cooked, rinsed, and drained
- 1½ cups shredded mozzarella cheese (6 ounces)
- 1 cup shredded mozzarella cheese (4 ounces)
- ¼ cup sliced pitted ripe olives
  Snipped parsley (optional)
  Green *or* red sweet pepper rings, (optional)

In a medium covered skillet cook sliced carrots, chopped onion, and minced garlic in hot olive or cooking oil till onion is tender but not brown. Stir in meatless spaghetti sauce, water, oregano, salt, and basil. Simmer, covered, about 15 minutes or till carrots are tender. If desired, reserve a few of the mushroom slices to garnish the top of the lasagna. Stir the remaining mushroom slices and the zucchini sticks into skillet. Cook, uncovered, about 5 minutes or till zucchini is tender.

Meanwhile, using paper toweling, squeeze any excess liquid from the thawed spinach. In a bowl stir together the beaten eggs, the drained cottage cheese or ricotta cheese, and Parmesan cheese.

Arrange a single layer of lasagna noodles in the bottom of a greased 12x7½x2-inch baking dish. Top noodles with ⅓ of the thawed spinach. Spread with ⅓ of the cottage or ricotta cheese mixture, then with ⅓ of the spaghetti sauce mixture. Sprinkle with ½ *cup* of the shredded mozzarella cheese. Repeat the layers 2 more times.

Bake, covered, in a 375° oven about 35 minutes or till heated through. Top lasagna with the 1 cup shredded mozzarella cheese, the sliced ripe olives, and the reserved mushroom slices, if desired. Return to oven for 3 minutes or till cheese is melted. Let stand 10 minutes before serving. If desired, garnish with snipped parsley and green or red sweet pepper rings. Makes 8 servings.

PEACH-YOGURT PIE

Pictured on pages 18 and 19
Provides 11% U.S. RDA of protein per serving —

1¼ cups fine graham cracker crumbs
  (about 18 square crackers)
¼ cup sugar
6 tablespoons butter *or*
  margarine, melted
1 3-ounce package peach-flavored
  gelatin
¼ cup water
2 slightly beaten egg yolks
2 3-ounce packages cream cheese,
  cubed and softened
1 8-ounce carton peach yogurt
2 egg whites
2 tablespoons sugar
1 medium peach, peeled, pitted,
  and sliced
  Lemon juice
  Unsweetened whipped cream
  (optional)
  Mint sprigs (optional)

For graham cracker crust, in a mixing bowl stir together graham cracker crumbs and the ¼ cup sugar. Stir the melted butter or margarine into the crumb mixture; toss thoroughly to combine. Turn the crumb-butter mixture into a 9-inch pie plate. Spread the crumb mixture evenly in the pie plate. Press onto the bottom and sides to form a firm, even crust. Bake in a 375° oven for 6 to 9 minutes or till edges are brown. Cool thoroughly on a wire rack before filling.

To make filling, place the peach gelatin in a saucepan. Stir in the water and beaten egg yolks. Cook and stir about 6 minutes or till the gelatin is dissolved and the mixture is slightly thickened. Remove from heat. Beat in softened cream cheese and peach yogurt till smooth. Slightly chill the mixture, stirring occasionally.

Using clean beaters, beat egg whites till soft peaks form. Gradually add the 2 ta-blespoons sugar, beating till stiff peaks form. When gelatin mixture is partially set to the consistency of unbeaten egg whites, fold egg whites into mixture. Brush the peach slices with a little lemon juice to prevent discoloration. If desired, reserve a few of the slices for a garnish; chop the remaining peaches and fold into the gelatin mixture. Chill till the mixture mounds when spooned.

Turn the chilled gelatin mixture into the cooled graham cracker crumb crust. Chill several hours or overnight till set. If desired, garnish the pie with whipped cream and the reserved peach slices or fresh mint sprigs. Cover and chill till serving time. Makes 8 servings.

APPLE-ALMOND SALAD

Pictured on pages 18 and 19
Provides 2% U.S. RDA of protein per serving —

¼ cup salad oil
2 tablespoons sugar
2 tablespoons malt vinegar
¼ teaspoon salt
⅛ teaspoon almond extract
6 cups torn mixed greens
3 medium apples, cut into
  wedges
1 cup thinly sliced celery
2 tablespoons sliced green
  onion
⅓ cup slivered almonds,
  toasted

For dressing, in a screw-top jar combine salad oil, sugar, malt vinegar, salt, and almond extract. Cover jar and shake well till sugar and salt dissolve. Chill in the refrigerator for several hours.

Before serving, in a large salad bowl combine mixed greens, apple wedges, sliced celery, and sliced green onion. Sprinkle with toasted almonds. Pour dressing over salad and toss gently to coat. Serve immediately. Makes 8 servings.

BREAKFAST MENU

Eggs-in-a-Puff

Cream-Cheese-Topped
Cantaloupe

Breakfast Drink

BREAKFAST DRINK

Provides 8% U.S. RDA of protein per serving —

  1   pint vanilla ice cream
1 ½ cups peach yogurt
  ¾ cup peach nectar, chilled
  ½ cup milk
  ½ teaspoon vanilla

In a blender container combine all ingredients. Cover and blend just till mixed. Pour into chilled glasses. Serves 6.

CREAM-CHEESE-TOPPED CANTALOUPE

Provides 3% U.S. RDA of protein per serving —

  1   3-ounce package cream
      cheese
  ½ teaspoon finely shredded
      orange peel
  2   tablespoons orange juice
  1   medium cantaloupe
1 ½ cups fresh *or* frozen unsweetened
      blueberries

Soften cream cheese; beat till fluffy. Stir in orange peel and juice. Seed and cut cantaloupe into wedges; top with berries. Pour cream cheese mixture over top. Makes 6 servings.

EGGS-IN-A-PUFF

Provides 29% U.S. RDA of protein per serving —

  ½ cup butter *or* margarine
  1   cup boiling water
  1   cup all-purpose flour
  ¼ teaspoon salt
  4   eggs
  8   beaten eggs
  ⅓ cup milk *or* light cream
  ¼ teaspoon salt
      Dash pepper
  ½ of a 10-ounce package frozen cut
      broccoli, cooked and drained,
      or ½ of a 6-ounce package
      frozen pea pods, thawed
  ½ small red *or* green sweet pepper,
      sliced or chopped
  2   tablespoons butter *or* margarine
  ½ cup shredded cheddar cheese
      (2 ounces)

To make the puff, melt the ½ cup butter or margarine in boiling water. Add flour and ¼ teaspoon salt all at once; stir vigorously. Cook and stir till mixture forms a ball that doesn't separate. Remove from heat; cool slightly (about 5 minutes). Add the 4 eggs, one at a time, beating after each till smooth. Spread batter over the bottom and up the sides of a greased 9-inch glass pie plate. Bake in a 400° oven about 25 minutes or till golden brown and puffy.

Meanwhile, use a fork to beat together the 8 beaten eggs, milk, ¼ teaspoon salt and pepper. Stir in broccoli or pea pods and red or green sweet pepper. Heat the 2 tablespoons butter or margarine in a skillet till just hot enough to make a drop of water sizzle. Pour in egg-vegetable mixture. Reduce heat to low. When egg mixture starts to set on the bottom and sides of the skillet, sprinkle with shredded cheddar cheese. Lift and fold the egg mixture with a spatula till eggs are cooked and cheese is melted. Spoon into the baked puff. Makes 6 servings.

22

Eggs-in-a-Puff, Cream-Cheese-Topped Cantaloupe,
and Breakfast Drink

BRUNCH MENU

Apple-Spice Soup
Brie Soufflé
Sliced Tomatoes
Easy Crescents with
Honey Butter
Café Orange

BRIE SOUFFLÉ

Provides 25% U.S. RDA of protein per serving—

- **2 tablespoons sliced green onion**
- **3 tablespoons butter *or* margarine**
- **3 tablespoons all-purpose flour**
- **¼ teaspoon salt**
- **¼ teaspoon ground nutmeg**
- **1 cup milk**
- **5 ounces Brie cheese, rind removed and cubed**
- **½ cup grated Parmesan cheese**
- **½ cup cauliflower flowerets, broken into small pieces**
- **¼ cup shredded carrot**
- **2 tablespoons snipped parsley**
- **5 egg yolks**
- **7 egg whites**

Attach a foil collar to a 2-quart soufflé dish. Measure enough foil to go around a 2-quart soufflé dish with a 2- to 3-inch overlap. Fold foil into thirds lengthwise. Lightly butter one side of the foil. Position foil around dish with buttered side in, letting collar extend 2 inches above top of dish; fasten with tape. Set aside.

In a medium saucepan cook onion in butter or margarine till tender but not brown. Stir in flour, salt, and ground nutmeg. Add milk all at once; cook and stir till thickened and bubbly. Cook and stir 1 to 2 minutes more. Add cubed Brie cheese and Parmesan cheese, stirring till the cheeses are melted. Remove from heat. Stir in cauliflower, carrot, and parsley.

In a small mixer bowl beat egg yolks about 5 minutes or till thick and lemon colored. Slowly add the Brie-Parmesan cheese mixture to the beaten yolks, stirring constantly. Cool slightly.

Using *clean* beaters, in a large mixer bowl beat egg whites at medium speed of electric mixer about 2½ minutes or till stiff peaks form (tips stand straight). Gradually pour the cheese-egg-yolk mixture over beaten egg whites, folding to combine mixtures. Pour into the prepared ungreased 2-quart soufflé dish. Use a metal spatula to trace a 1-inch-deep circle through the mixture about 1 inch from the edge. Bake in a 350° oven about 40 minutes or till a knife inserted near center comes out clean. *Do not* open oven door during baking. Test soufflé at the end of the suggested baking time while soufflé is still in the oven. Gently peel off collar. Serve immediately. Makes 6 servings.

CAFÉ ORANGE

Provides 1% U.S. RDA of protein per serving—

- **½ cup ground coffee**
- **2 teaspoons finely shredded orange peel**
- **3 cups water**
- **½ cup Amaretto liqueur**
- **½ cup whipping cream, whipped**

Combine coffee and orange peel; in a 6-cup percolator brew for 6 to 8 minutes with 3 cups water. Remove and discard coffee grounds. Stir Amaretto into brewed coffee. Pour into 6 coffee cups. Top *each* with a dollop of whipped cream. Makes 6 servings.

EASY CRESCENTS WITH HONEY BUTTER

Provides 6% U.S. RDA of protein per serving—

3¾ to 4¼ cups all-purpose flour
  ⅓ cup nonfat dry milk powder
  1 package active dry yeast
  1 cup warm water (115° to 120°)
  ½ cup butter *or* margarine,
    softened
  ½ teaspoon salt
  2 tablespoons butter *or*
    margarine, melted
  1 egg
  1 tablespoon water
  ¼ cup honey
  ½ teaspoon finely shredded lemon
    peel
  ½ cup butter *or* margarine,
    softened

In a large mixer bowl combine 2 *cups* of the flour, the nonfat dry milk, and the yeast. Combine warm water, ½ cup butter or margarine, and salt. Add to flour mixture. Beat at low speed of electric mixer for ½ minute, scraping bowl. Beat 3 minutes at high speed. Stir in as much of the remaining flour as you can mix in with a spoon. Turn out onto a lightly floured surface. Knead in enough of the remaining flour to make a moderately stiff dough that is smooth and elastic (6 to 8 minutes total). Shape into a ball. Place in a lightly greased bowl; turn once to grease surface. Cover; let rise in a warm place till double (about 45 minutes).

Punch down; divide dough into three equal portions. Cover; let rest 10 minutes. Roll out *one* portion of dough into a 12-inch circle. Brush with *some* of the 2 tablespoons melted butter or margarine. Cut the circle of dough into 12 wedges. Roll up *each* wedge loosely, starting from the wide end. Place rolls 2 to 3 inches apart, with points down, on an ungreased baking sheet. Repeat rolling, cutting, and shaping rolls with two remaining portions. Cover with clear plastic wrap and refrigerate overnight.

The next day, remove rolls from the refrigerator. Let stand 30 minutes. Beat together egg and the 1 tablespoon water till well combined. Brush egg mixture over rolls. Bake in a 375° oven for 12 to 15 minutes or till golden brown.

To make honey butter, gradually add honey and lemon peel to the remaining ½ cup softened butter or margarine, stirring till well combined. (If desired, the butter or margarine, honey, and lemon peel can be whipped together with an electric mixer.) Serve honey butter with the rolls. Makes 36 rolls (18 servings).

APPLE-SPICE SOUP

Provides 3% U.S. RDA of protein per serving—

2½ cups apple juice *or* apple cider
  2 cups dry white wine
  2 cups water
  1 8-ounce package mixed dried
    fruits, snipped
  1 cup dried apples, cut into
    quarters
  2 tablespoons quick-cooking
    tapioca
  ½ teaspoon ground allspice
  ¼ teaspoon ground cloves
    Dried apple rings (optional)

To make soup, in a 3-quart saucepan combine apple juice, wine, water, mixed dried fruits, dried apples, tapioca, allspice, and cloves. Let stand for 5 minutes. Bring fruit mixture to boiling; reduce heat. Cover and simmer 15 minutes. Remove from heat. Cool to room temperature.

Chill soup in the refrigerator for several hours or overnight. Serve soup cold. Garnish with apple rings, if desired. Makes 6 servings.

Note: If desired, serve the soup warm.

DINNER MENU

Fried Rice Patties with
Peanut Sauce

Tropical Spinach Salad

Yogurt-Rye Breadsticks

Chocolate-Almond Mousse

Beverage

TROPICAL SPINACH SALAD

Provides 4% U.S. RDA of protein per serving—

3 tablespoons salad oil
¼ teaspoon finely shredded
    orange peel
2 tablespoons orange
    juice
1 teaspoon lemon juice
¼ teaspoon dry mustard
⅛ teaspoon salt
3 cups torn fresh spinach
1 11-ounce can mandarin orange
    sections, drained
½ cup sliced fresh mushrooms
1 tablespoon sesame seed,
    toasted

For salad dressing, in a screw-top jar combine salad oil, orange peel, orange juice, lemon juice, dry mustard, and salt. Cover jar and shake well. Chill for several hours.

Before serving, in a salad bowl combine torn spinach, mandarin orange sections, fresh mushroom slices, and toasted sesame seed. Pour dressing over salad; toss together. Makes 3 servings.

FRIED RICE PATTIES WITH PEANUT SAUCE

Pictured on page 43

Provides 30% U.S. RDA of protein per serving—

2 cups water
⅔ cup *medium or short grain* rice
1 beaten egg
¼ cup finely chopped onion
¼ cup finely chopped green pepper
¼ cup finely chopped peanuts
¼ cup finely chopped shelled
    sunflower seed
3 tablespoons toasted wheat germ
¼ teaspoon salt
⅛ teaspoon pepper
½ cup drained, crushed pineapple
¼ cup chunk-style peanut butter
¼ cup dairy sour cream
1 teaspoon soy sauce
½ teaspoon lemon juice
2 tablespoons cooking oil

In a medium saucepan bring water to boiling; add rice. Return to boiling; reduce heat and simmer about 20 minutes or till rice is tender and water is absorbed. While rice is still *warm,* add the beaten egg, chopped onion, green pepper, peanuts, sunflower seed, toasted wheat germ, salt, and pepper; mix well.

Meanwhile, for peanut sauce, combine drained pineapple, peanut butter, dairy sour cream, soy sauce, and lemon juice; set aside.

Using about ½ *cup* for *each* patty, shape rice mixture into 6 patties about ¾ inch thick. In a skillet, cook patties in hot cooking oil, uncovered, over medium heat about 3 minutes. Gently turn patties; dollop with peanut sauce. Cook about 3 minutes longer or till patties are golden. Makes 3 servings.

Note: If desired, cook patties without dolloping with peanut sauce. Pass the peanut sauce at serving time.

YOGURT-RYE BREADSTICKS

Provides 5% U.S. RDA of protein per serving—

¾ cup all-purpose flour
1 package active dry yeast
¼ cup milk
2 tablespoons butter *or* margarine
1 tablespoon brown sugar
½ cup plain yogurt
1 cup rye flour
½ cup all-purpose flour

Combine the ¾ cup all-purpose flour and the yeast. Heat milk, butter or margarine, brown sugar, and 1 teaspoon *salt* till warm (115° to 120°) and butter or margarine is almost melted, stirring constantly.

Add the warm milk mixture to flour mixture. Add plain yogurt. Beat at low speed of electric mixer for ½ minute, scraping the sides of the bowl constantly. Beat 3 minutes at high speed of electric mixer. Stir in as much of the rye flour as you can mix in with a spoon.

Turn batter out onto a lightly floured surface. Knead in the rye flour and enough of the ½ cup all-purpose flour to make a stiff dough that is smooth and elastic (8 to 10 minutes total). Shape dough into a ball. Place in a lightly greased bowl; turn once to grease surface of dough. Cover; let rise in a warm place till double (1 to 1¼ hours).

Punch dough down; turn out onto a lightly floured surface. Divide dough into 4 portions. Cover and let rest 10 minutes. Divide each portion into six pieces. Roll *each* piece into a rope 8 inches long. Place ropes about 2 inches apart on greased baking sheets. Cover; let rise in a warm place till nearly double (about 30 minutes). Bake in a 375° oven for 10 minutes. Reduce temperature to 300°; bake 20 to 25 minutes longer or till brown and crisp. Makes 24 breadsticks (12 servings).

CHOCOLATE-ALMOND MOUSSE

Provides 15% U.S. RDA of protein per serving—

2 tablespoons sugar
2 teaspoons unsweetened cocoa powder
1 teaspoon unflavored gelatin
1 teaspoon instant coffee crystals
Dash salt
¾ cup water
¼ cup milk
1 beaten egg yolk
1 egg white
½ teaspoon vanilla
⅛ teaspoon cream of tartar
½ of a 4½-ounce container frozen whipped dessert topping, thawed
1 tablespoon slivered almonds, toasted

In a small saucepan stir together sugar, unsweetened cocoa powder, gelatin, coffee crystals, and salt. Stir in water, milk, and beaten egg yolk. Cook and stir 2 to 3 minutes or till mixture is slightly thickened. *Do not boil.* Remove from heat. Chill gelatin mixture to the consistency of corn syrup, stirring occasionally.

Beat the egg white with the vanilla and cream of tartar till stiff peaks form (tips curl over). When the gelatin is partially set to the consistency of unbeaten egg whites, fold the stiff-beaten egg whites into the gelatin mixture. Fold the thawed whipped dessert topping into the egg-white-gelatin mixture.

Spoon the mixture into three individual parfait glasses or sherbet glasses. Sprinkle *each* serving with toasted slivered almonds. Chill in the refrigerator several hours or overnight, till the mixture is set. Makes 3 servings.

Spinach Crescents, Whole Wheat Cookies, Barley-Cheese Soup (see recipe, page 49), and Yogurt Ambrosia

LUNCH MENU

Barley-Cheese Soup
(see recipe, page 49)
Spinach Crescents
Yogurt Ambrosia
Whole Wheat Cookies
Beverage

WHOLE WHEAT COOKIES

Provides 3% U.S. RDA of protein per serving—

½ cup raisins
¾ cup whole wheat flour
½ teaspoon baking soda
¼ teaspoon ground nutmeg
¼ teaspoon ground cinnamon
½ cup shortening
½ cup packed brown sugar
¼ cup granulated sugar
1 egg
1 cup quick-cooking rolled oats
¼ cup chopped walnuts

Cover raisins with water. Bring to boiling; remove from heat. Cover; let stand 5 minutes. Drain. Put raisins through the fine blade of a food grinder. Set aside. Stir together whole wheat flour, baking soda, nutmeg, cinnamon, and ½ teaspoon *salt*.

Cream shortening and sugars till fluffy. Beat in eggs. Add flour mixture; beat till combined. Stir in oats, nuts, and ground raisins. Drop by rounded teaspoonfuls onto a greased cookie sheet. Bake in a 350° oven 9 to 10 minutes. Cool for 1 to 2 minutes; remove to a wire rack. Makes 40 cookies (20 servings).

SPINACH CRESCENTS

Provides 11% U.S. RDA of protein per serving—

1 tablespoon slivered almonds
1 cup torn fresh spinach, steamed
3 tablespoons grated Parmesan cheese
2 teaspoons finely chopped onion
2 teaspoons cooking oil
1 package (8) refrigerated crescent rolls
Sesame seed

In a covered blender container, blend almonds till finely ground. Add spinach, Parmesan cheese, onion, and oil. Cover; blend till a paste forms, stopping and pushing mixture down as necessary.

Unroll rolls and separate into triangles. Spread *each* triangle with about *2 teaspoons* of the spinach mixture. Roll up. Place, point down, on an ungreased baking sheet. Sprinkle with sesame seed. Bake in a 375° oven 10 to 13 minutes. Makes 8 rolls. (4 servings).

YOGURT AMBROSIA

Provides 5% U.S. RDA of protein per serving—

1 cup seedless green grapes
1 11-ounce can mandarin orange sections, drained
1 small apple, cut into bite-size chunks
1 small banana, sliced
¼ cup broken pecans
¾ cup plain yogurt
1 tablespoon honey
⅛ teaspoon ground cinnamon
¼ cup coconut, toasted

Halve grapes. Combine grapes, orange sections, apple, banana, and pecans. Stir together yogurt, honey, and cinnamon; fold into fruit. Cover; chill for several hours. To serve, spoon mixture into individual dishes; top with coconut. Serves 4.

29

MEATLESS MAIN·DISHES

Casseroles. Soups. Stews. Main-dish pies. Quiches. Meal-size salads and sandwiches. They're all here in this chapter, and they're all tasty, attractive, filling, and meatless. Whether you're looking for a sandwich idea for a nutritious busy-day lunch or a hearty casserole for dinner, you'll find recipes that you'll want to serve again and again.

*Apple-Cheese Muffins, Zucchini-Cheese Turnovers,
Carrot-Cauliflower Pasta Toss, Three-Vegetable Pie,
Rice Puffs with Vegetable Sauce, and Tofu-Fruit Salad
(See Index for recipe pages.)*

TOP·OF·THE·RANGE

RICE PUFFS WITH VEGETABLE SAUCE

Pictured on pages 30 and 31

Provides 26% U.S. RDA of protein per serving—

    3 cups cooked short *or* medium
        grain rice, cooled
    3 slightly beaten eggs
  1/3 cup all-purpose flour
  1/2 teaspoon salt
  1/4 teaspoon pepper
    3 ounces American cheese, cut into
        1/2-inch cubes
  1/2 cup finely crushed saltine
        crackers
      Cooking oil
    2 tablespoons chopped green
        pepper
    2 tablespoons chopped onion
    2 tablespoons shredded carrot
    2 tablespoons butter *or* margarine
    2 tablespoons all-purpose flour
1 1/4 cups milk

Combine first 5 ingredients. With wet hands, shape about 2 *tablespoons* of the rice mixture around a cheese cube. Repeat with remaining rice and cheese. Roll *each* in crackers. In a skillet cook 4 or 5 rice puffs in 1/2 inch of hot oil (365°) about 3 minutes or till golden, turning once; drain. Keep warm; repeat.

For sauce, cook green pepper, onion, and carrot in butter till tender. Stir in the 2 tablespoons flour, 1/2 teaspoon *salt,* and dash *pepper.* Add milk. Cook and stir till thickened and bubbly. Cook and stir 1 to 2 minutes more. Add any remaining cheese cubes; stirring till melted. To serve, top rice puffs with sauce. Serves 4.

CHEESE AND RICE PATTIES

Provides 29% U.S. RDA of protein per serving—

    3 tablespoons chopped green
        pepper
    1 tablespoon butter *or* margarine
    1 8-ounce can tomato sauce
    2 tablespoons snipped parsley
  1/2 teaspoon dried thyme, crushed
  1/2 of a 10-ounce package frozen
        chopped spinach
    1 beaten egg
    2 cups hot cooked brown rice
    1 cup cream-style cottage cheese,
        drained
  1/2 cup shredded mozzarella cheese
  1/2 cup fine dry bread crumbs
  1/4 cup grated Parmesan cheese
  1/4 teaspoon ground nutmeg
    1 beaten egg
  1/2 cup fine dry bread crumbs
    2 tablespoons cooking oil

For sauce, cook green pepper in butter or margarine till tender. Stir in tomato sauce, parsley, and thyme. Bring to boiling; reduce heat. Cover and simmer about 10 minutes, stirring occasionally. Cook spinach according to package directions. Drain well. Combine 1 egg, spinach, rice, drained cottage cheese, mozzarella cheese, 1/2 cup bread crumbs, Parmesan cheese, and nutmeg. Shape into five patties about 3/4 inch thick. Combine 1 egg and 1 tablespoon *water.* Dip patties into egg mixture then into the 1/2 cup bread crumbs. Cook in hot oil about 4 minutes on each side or till golden. Pass sauce. Serves 5.

32

HOMINY-RICE SKILLET

Provides 29% U.S. RDA of protein per serving —

½ **cup chopped onion**
1 **tablespoon cooking oil**
1 **16-ounce can tomatoes, cut up**
1 **16-ounce can hominy, drained**
1¾ **cups water**
1 **cup brown rice**
3 **tablespoons canned green chili**
   peppers, rinsed, seeded, and
   chopped
1 **teaspoon ground coriander**
½ **teaspoon salt**
1 **cup shredded cheddar cheese**
½ **cup pumpkin seed, toasted**

In a skillet cook onion in hot oil till tender but not brown. Add *undrained* tomatoes, hominy, water, *uncooked* rice, chili peppers, coriander, and salt. Bring to boiling. Reduce heat; cover and simmer 50 minutes or till rice is tender. Sprinkle cheese atop; cover and cook 1 to 2 minutes more or till cheese is melted. Top with pumpkin seed. Serves 4.

LENTIL PATTIES

Provides 25% U.S. RDA of protein per serving —

¾ **cup dry lentils**
½ **cup pumpkin seed, toasted**
1 **slightly beaten egg**
⅓ **cup fine dry bread crumbs**
½ **cup finely chopped onion**
¼ **cup chopped walnuts**
¼ **cup snipped parsley**
¼ **cup chili sauce**
½ **teaspoon salt**
⅛ **teaspoon pepper**
2 **tablespoons butter *or* margarine**
½ **cup dairy sour cream**

Combine lentils and 3 cups *water;* bring to boiling. Reduce heat; cover and simmer 45 to 50 minutes or till tender. Drain. Mash cooked lentils. Chop toasted pumpkin seed. Combine egg, mashed lentils, pumpkin seeds, bread crumbs, onion, walnuts, parsley, chili sauce, salt, and pepper. Shape into five patties about ¾ inch thick. Cook in butter over medium heat about 4 minutes on each side or till golden brown. Top each patty with a dollop of sour cream. Makes 5 servings.

FRIED POTATO CAKES

Provides 32% U.S. RDA of protein per serving —

¼ **cup whole wheat flour**
1 **beaten egg**
2 **teaspoons cooking oil**
2 **cups coarsely shredded potatoes**
3 **tablespoons finely chopped onion**
3 **tablespoons shelled sunflower**
   seed
2 **tablespoons fine dry bread**
   crumbs
2 **tablespoons butter *or* margarine**
1 **tablespoon whole wheat flour**
½ **cup milk**
½ **cup shredded cheddar cheese**
2 **tablespoons shelled sunflower**
   seed

In a bowl combine flour and ⅛ teaspoon *salt*. Combine egg and oil; stir into flour mixture just till moistened. Stir in potatoes, onion, the 3 tablespoons sunflower seed, and bread crumbs. Shape into 4 patties about ½ inch thick. Cook patties in *1 tablespoon* of the butter over medium heat about 3 minutes on each side or till golden brown. Remove from skillet. Keep warm.

For sauce, melt the remaining 1 tablespoon butter in a saucepan. Stir in the 1 tablespoon flour and ⅛ teaspoon *salt*. Add milk all at once. Cook and stir till thickened and bubbly. Cook and stir 1 to 2 minutes more. Add cheese, stirring till melted. Top each patty with some of the sauce and some of the 2 tablespoons sunflower seed. Serves 2.

33

CRUNCHY RICE PATTIES

Provides 37% U.S. RDA of protein per serving —

1 1/4 cups water
1/2 cup brown rice
2 beaten eggs
3/4 cup fine dry bread crumbs
1/2 cup sliced green onion
1/2 cup shelled sunflower seed
1 tablespoon chopped pimiento
1/2 teaspoon ground sage
1/4 teaspoon salt
2 tablespoons cooking oil
4 teaspoons butter *or* margarine
2 tablespoons all-purpose flour
1/8 teaspoon salt
1 cup milk
1/2 cup shredded cheddar cheese
    (2 ounces)
    Snipped parsley (optional)

In a small saucepan bring the water to boiling; add the *uncooked* rice and return to boiling. Reduce heat; simmer, covered, 45 to 50 minutes or till the water is absorbed and the rice is tender.

In a medium bowl combine cooked rice, beaten eggs, dry bread crumbs, green onion, sunflower seed, pimiento, sage, and the 1/4 teaspoon salt. Shape the rice mixture into six 1/2-inch-thick patties. In a large skillet over medium heat, fry the rice patties in the hot cooking oil till golden brown, allowing 3 to 4 minutes per side.

Meanwhile, to make cheese sauce, in a small saucepan melt the butter or margarine. Stir in the all-purpose flour and the 1/8 teaspoon salt. Add the milk all at once. Cook and stir till the mixture is thickened and bubbly. Cook and stir 1 to 2 minutes more. Stir in the shredded cheddar cheese till melted. Serve the cheese sauce over the rice patties. If desired, sprinkle rice patties with snipped parsley. Makes 3 servings.

EGGS A LA SUISSE

Provides 32% U.S. RDA of protein per serving —

3 tablespoons chopped green
    pepper
2 tablespoons chopped onion
2 tablespoons butter *or*
    margarine
2 tablespoons all-purpose flour
1 tablespoon horseradish mustard
1/4 teaspoon salt
1/4 teaspoon pepper
1/8 teaspoon dried oregano,
    crushed
1/8 teaspoon dried thyme, crushed
1 cup milk
6 eggs
3 English muffins, split and
    toasted
6 slices cheddar cheese
    (4 ounces)
6 slices Swiss cheese (4 ounces)
    Paprika

For sauce, in a saucepan cook green pepper and onion in butter or margarine till tender. Stir in flour, horseradish mustard, salt, pepper, oregano, and thyme. Add milk all at once. Cook and stir till mixture is thickened and bubbly. Cook and stir 1 to 2 minutes more. Cover and keep warm.

Lightly grease a 12-inch skillet. In the skillet heat 1 1/2 inches of water to boiling; reduce heat to simmer. Break 1 of the eggs into a sauce dish; carefully slide egg into simmering water. Repeat with remaining eggs, keeping them separate in the skillet. Simmer, uncovered, over low heat for 3 to 5 minutes or to desired doneness. (*Do not* let water boil.)

Meanwhile, top each muffin half with a slice *each* of cheddar and Swiss cheese. Broil till cheese melts. When eggs are done, lift out with a slotted spoon; place one egg on *each* cheese-topped muffin half. Spoon sauce over each. Sprinkle paprika atop. Makes 6 servings.

SPICY BEAN TOSTADAS

Provides 27% U.S. RDA of protein per serving—

1 15½-ounce can red kidney beans, drained
1 14½-ounce can yellow hominy, drained
1 10-ounce can tomatoes and green chili peppers
1 8-ounce can tomato sauce
½ cup sliced celery
1 tablespoon snipped parsley
½ teaspoon sugar
1 tablespoon cold water
1 teaspoon cornstarch

• • •

Cooking oil
4 10-inch flour tortillas
1 cup shredded cheddar cheese (4 ounces)
1 cup chopped lettuce
Chili salsa *or* taco sauce (optional)

In a 2-quart saucepan combine drained kidney beans, drained hominy, tomatoes and green chili peppers, tomato sauce, sliced celery, snipped parsley, and sugar. Bring the tomato and bean mixture to boiling. Reduce heat; simmer, covered, for 10 minutes. Combine the cold water and the cornstarch; stir into the tomato and bean mixture. Cook and stir till the mixture is thickened and bubbly. Cook and stir for 1 to 2 minutes longer. Meanwhile, in a heavy skillet heat ¼ inch of cooking oil. Fry the flour tortillas, one at a time, in the hot oil for 20 to 40 seconds per side or till they are crisp and golden. Drain fried tortillas on paper toweling; wrap in foil and keep warm in a 250° oven while frying the remainder.

Place warm tortillas on dinner plates. Divide the tomato mixture evenly among tortillas; sprinkle with the shredded cheddar cheese and the chopped lettuce. Pass chili salsa or taco sauce, if desired. Makes 4 servings.

CHEESE AND BEAN BURRITOS

Provides 31% U.S. RDA of protein per serving—

1¼ cups dry pinto beans
3 cups water
1 small onion, chopped (¼ cup)
¼ cup chili salsa
1 clove garlic, minced
¾ teaspoon salt
6 10-inch flour tortillas
1 small tomato, chopped
1½ cups shredded Monterey Jack cheese (6 ounces)
Cooking oil
½ cup dairy sour cream
2 medium avocados, sliced (optional)

Rinse the pinto beans. In a 3-quart saucepan combine the pinto beans and water. Bring the beans to boiling. Reduce heat; simmer, covered, for 2½ to 3 hours or till the beans are very tender. Mash beans completely. Add the onion, chili salsa, garlic, and salt. Cook the bean mixture, uncovered, over medium heat about 5 minutes or till thick, stirring often.

Wrap tortillas tightly in foil; heat in a 350° oven for 10 minutes or till the tortillas are warm. Lightly salt the chopped tomato. Spoon ⅓ cup of the bean mixture on each warm tortilla near one edge. Top with shredded cheese and chopped tomato. Fold the edge nearest the filling up and over the filling just till the mixture is covered. Fold in two sides as for an envelope, then roll up.

In a skillet containing ½ inch hot cooking oil, fry *each* filled tortilla about 1 minute on each side or till golden brown. Keep warm in a 300° oven while frying the remaining filled tortillas. Top fried filled tortillas with a dollop of sour cream and several avocado slices, if desired. Makes 6 servings.

35

GARDEN VEGETABLE STIR-FRY

Provides 31% U.S. RDA of protein per serving —

- 16 ounces fresh tofu (bean curd)
- 3 small carrots, cut into thirds
- 4 ounces fresh broccoli, cut into 1-inch pieces (1½ cups)
- 2 green onions, bias-sliced into 1½-inch lengths
- ½ cup chicken broth
- 2 tablespoons soy sauce
- 1 tablespoon cornstarch
- 1 tablespoon cooking oil
- 1 clove garlic, minced
- ½ teaspoon grated fresh gingerroot
- 1 cup sliced crookneck squash
- 1 medium tomato, cut into thin wedges
- 2 cups hot cooked brown rice
- ½ cup peanuts

Place tofu in a double thickness of cheesecloth or paper toweling. Press gently to extract as much moisture as possible. Cut tofu into ½-inch cubes; set aside.

In a covered saucepan cook carrots and broccoli in boiling salted water for 3 minutes. Add onions. Cook 2 minutes more; drain well. Stir together chicken broth, soy sauce, and cornstarch; set aside.

Preheat a wok or large skillet over high heat; add cooking oil. Stir-fry cubed tofu 3 to 4 minutes or till golden. Remove and set aside. Add more oil, if necessary. Stir-fry garlic and gingerroot for 30 seconds. Add squash; stir-fry 2 to 3 minutes. Remove; set aside.

Stir broth mixture; pour into wok. Cook and stir till thickened and bubbly. Cook and stir 1 to 2 minutes more. Return tofu and vegetables to wok. Add tomatoes; cover and cook 1 to 2 minutes or till heated through. Serve over hot brown rice. Top with peanuts. If desired, pass additional soy sauce. Serves 4.

PEPPERY TOFU WITH CASHEWS

Provides 31% U.S. RDA of protein per serving —

- 3 tablespoons soy sauce
- 2 teaspoons cornstarch
- ⅓ cup water
- 2 tablespoons dry sherry
- 1 teaspoon sugar
- 1 teaspoon grated fresh gingerroot
- ½ teaspoon crushed red pepper
- 16 ounces fresh tofu (bean curd)
- 1 tablespoon cooking oil
- 16 ounces fresh asparagus *or* one 8-ounce package frozen asparagus spears, thawed
- 4 green onions
- 1 cup cashews
- 1 11-ounce can mandarin orange sections, drained
- 2 cups hot cooked brown rice

In a small bowl combine 3 tablespoons soy sauce with cornstarch; stir in water, sherry, sugar, gingerroot, red pepper, and ½ teaspoon *salt*. Set aside.

Place tofu in a double thickness of cheesecloth or paper toweling. Press gently to extract as much moisture as possible. Cut tofu into ½-inch cubes.

Preheat a wok or large skillet over high heat; add cooking oil. Stir-fry tofu 3 to 4 minutes or till golden. Remove from wok. Add more oil, if necessary. Bias-slice asparagus and green onion into 1-inch lengths; stir-fry 2 to 3 minutes or till crisp-tender. Remove from wok. Add cashews to wok; stir-fry 1 to 2 minutes or till golden. Stir soy mixture; stir into cashews. Cook and stir till thickened and bubbly. Cook and stir 1 to 2 minutes more. Return tofu and vegetables to wok; cover and cook 1 minute more. Stir orange sections into tofu mixture; heat through. Serve over hot rice. If desired, pass additional soy sauce. Serves 4.

36

Peppery Tofu with Cashews

BROWN RICE AND TOFU STIR-FRY

Provides 30% U.S. RDA of protein per serving—

1 1/3 cups water
1/2 cup brown rice
16 ounces fresh tofu (bean curd)
3 tablespoons cooking oil
1 medium carrot, thinly
    bias-sliced
4 green onions, bias-sliced into
    1-inch lengths
1 small green pepper, cut into
    bite-size pieces
1 clove garlic, minced
1/2 teaspoon grated gingerroot
1 cup broken walnuts
1 cup fresh pea pods *or* one
    6-ounce package frozen
    pea pods, thawed
1 cup cherry tomatoes, halved
2 tablespoons soy sauce

In a saucepan bring water and 1/4 teaspoon *salt* to boiling. Stir in rice. Reduce heat; cover and simmer for 45 to 50 minutes or till rice is tender. Set aside.

Place tofu in a double thickness of cheesecloth or paper toweling. Press gently to extract as much moisture as possible. Cut tofu into 1/2-inch cubes.

Preheat a wok or large skillet over high heat; add cooking oil. Stir-fry cubed tofu 3 to 4 minutes or till golden. Remove from wok. Add carrot; stir-fry 2 minutes. Add green onion, green pepper, garlic, and gingerroot; stir-fry 2 minutes more. Remove vegetable mixture from skillet; add walnuts and stir-fry 1 to 2 minutes or till nuts are toasted.

Add more oil, if necessary. Add pea pods, cooked rice, tofu, and vegetable mixture to wok or skillet. Cook and stir 2 minutes more. Add cherry tomato halves. Cover and cook 1 minute or till tomatoes are heated through. Stir in soy sauce. Serves 4.

BULGUR AND VEGETABLE STIR-FRY

Provides 26% U.S. RDA of protein per serving—

2 cups water
2 tablespoons instant beef
    bouillon granules
1 cup bulgur wheat
2 medium carrots, thinly bias-
    sliced
1/2 pound broccoli, cut into
    1-inch pieces
    Water
    Salt
1 tablespoon cold water
1 teaspoon cornstarch
1 tablespoon soy sauce
1 tablespoon cooking oil
3/4 cup cashews
4 green onions, bias-sliced into
    1-inch lengths
2 small tomatoes, cut into thin
    wedges

Combine the 2 cups water and instant beef bouillon granules; heat till warm. Pour bouillon over bulgur and let the mixture stand 1 hour. Drain, pressing out any excess liquid. Set aside.

Meanwhile, cook carrots and broccoli in a small amount of boiling salted water for 5 minutes; drain. Combine the 1 table-spoon cold water and the cornstarch; stir in the 1 tablespoon soy sauce.

Preheat a wok or large skillet over high heat. Add cooking oil. Stir-fry sliced carrots, broccoli pieces, cashews, and sliced green onions for 2 minutes or till carrots are crisp-tender.

Add soy sauce mixture; cook and stir till thickened and bubbly. Cook and stir 1 to 2 minutes more. Add tomato wedges; cover and cook 1 minute or till tomatoes are heated through. Add bulgur and toss gently; heat through. If desired, pass additional soy sauce. Makes 3 servings.

EGGS A L'ASPARAGUS

Provides 27% U.S. RDA of protein per serving—

12 ounces fresh asparagus *or* one
   8-ounce package frozen
   asparagus spears
 2 tablespoons butter *or* margarine
 2 tablespoons all-purpose flour
½ teaspoon salt
   Dash pepper
1¼ cups milk
½ cup shredded American cheese
   (2 ounces)
 4 hard-cooked eggs, sliced
 4 slices toast
   Paprika

Cook whole fresh asparagus spears in a small amount of boiling salted water 10 to 15 minutes or till tender. (*Or,* cook frozen asparagus according to package directions.) Drain. Melt butter over low heat; stir in flour, salt, and pepper. Add milk all at once; cook and stir till thickened and bubbly. Cook and stir 1 to 2 minutes more. Add cheese, stirring till melted. Fold in egg slices. Arrange hot asparagus spears on toast. Spoon egg mixture over asparagus. Sprinkle with paprika. Serves 4.

SCRAMBLED EGGS WITH BROCCOLI

Provides 32% U.S. RDA of protein per serving—

½ of a 10-ounce package frozen cut
   broccoli
¼ cup chopped onion
 2 tablespoons butter *or* margarine
 6 eggs
½ cup shredded mozzarella cheese
¼ cup milk
 2 tablespoons chopped pimiento
½ teaspoon chili powder

Cook broccoli according to package directions. Drain. In a 10-inch skillet cook onion in butter till tender but not brown. Add broccoli to onion in skillet. Beat together eggs, *half* of the cheese, milk, pimiento, chili powder, ¼ teaspoon *salt,* and dash *pepper.* Pour over the broccoli mixture in skillet. Cook, without stirring, over medium heat till eggs begin to set on bottom and sides of skillet. Lift and fold eggs with a spatula so the uncooked portion flows underneath. Continue lifting and folding about 5 minutes or till eggs are cooked through but are still glossy and moist. Top with remaining cheese. Serves 3.

HUEVOS RANCHEROS

Provides 31% U.S. RDA of protein per serving—

¼ cup cooking oil
 4 6-inch tortillas
½ cup chopped onion
 1 16-ounce can tomatoes, cut up
 2 canned green chili peppers,
   rinsed, seeded, and chopped
½ teaspoon chili powder
⅛ teaspoon garlic powder
 8 eggs
½ cup shredded Monterey Jack *or*
   American cheese

In a 10-inch skillet heat oil. Fry tortillas, one at a time, in oil about 30 seconds on each side or till crisp and golden. Drain. Wrap in foil and keep warm in a 250° oven. In the same skillet cook onion in the remaining oil till tender. Add *undrained* tomatoes, chili peppers, chili powder, garlic powder, and ¼ teaspoon *salt.* Simmer 5 to 10 minutes or till slightly thickened. Break an egg into a small dish. Carefully slide egg into hot tomato mixture. Repeat with remaining eggs. Season with salt and pepper. Cover and cook over low heat 3 to 5 minutes or till eggs are the desired doneness. To serve, place 2 eggs and some tomato mixture on each tortilla. Top with cheese. Serves 4.

Garden Frittata Parmesan

GARDEN FRITTATA PARMESAN

Provides 30% U.S. RDA of protein per serving —

2 cups fresh broccoli flowerets, chopped, *or* one 10-ounce package frozen chopped broccoli
8 beaten eggs
¼ cup grated Parmesan cheese
¼ cup milk
1 tablespoon all-purpose flour
½ teaspoon dried basil *or* thyme, crushed
1 tablespoon cooking oil
6 thin tomato slices
Cooking oil
1 tablespoon grated Parmesan cheese
Dairy sour cream
Snipped chives

In a saucepan cook fresh broccoli in boiling salted water, covered, 8 to 10 minutes. (*Or,* cook frozen broccoli according to package directions.) Drain. Combine eggs, the ¼ cup Parmesan cheese, milk, flour, basil or thyme, ¼ teaspoon *salt,* and ¼ teaspoon *pepper;* mix well. Add broccoli. In a 10-inch oven-going skillet or omelet pan, heat the oil; swirl to coat the bottom and sides of the pan. Pour the broccoli-egg mixture into the hot skillet. Cook over medium-low heat, lifting edges occasionally to allow the uncooked portion to flow underneath. Cook about 4 minutes, or till edges begin to set and bottom is lightly browned. Place pan under the broiler, 4 to 5 inches from the heat, for 2 minutes or till set. Top with tomato slices; brush tomato slices lightly with oil. Sprinkle with the 1 tablespoon Parmesan cheese. Broil about ½ minute more or till tomatoes are heated. Cut into wedges to serve. Top each serving with a dollop of sour cream; sprinkle with chives. Serves 4.

MEXICALI POACHED EGGS

Provides 28% U.S. RDA of protein per serving —

½ cup sliced fresh mushrooms
¼ cup chopped green pepper
2 tablespoons chopped onion
2 tablespoons butter *or* margarine
1 tablespoon all-purpose flour
1¼ cups milk
1 cup shredded American cheese (4 ounces)
2 tablespoons chopped pimiento
Dash bottled hot pepper sauce
½ cup dairy sour cream
6 eggs
3 English muffins, split and toasted
½ cup shredded American cheese (2 ounces)
Paprika

For sauce, in a 10-inch skillet cook mushrooms, green pepper, and onion in butter or margarine till mushrooms are tender. Stir in flour. Add milk all at once. Cook and stir till thickened and bubbly. Cook and stir 1 to 2 minutes more. Add the 1 cup shredded cheese, pimiento, and hot pepper sauce, stirring till cheese is melted. Gradually stir *some* of the hot mixture into the sour cream. Return the sour cream mixture to skillet.

Break *one* egg into a small dish. Slide egg into skillet, holding edge of dish as close to the sauce as possible. Repeat with remaining eggs.

Simmer eggs, covered, for 3 to 5 minutes or till eggs are just soft-cooked.

Top each toasted English muffin half with an egg; spoon sauce over. Top eggs with ½ cup cheese and a little paprika. Makes 6 servings.

41

CHEESE FRITTATINE

Provides 29% U.S. RDA of protein per serving —

- 3 tablespoons butter *or* margarine
- 5 medium tomatoes, peeled and chopped
- ½ teaspoon salt
- ½ teaspoon dried basil, crushed
- ½ teaspoon dried oregano, crushed
- ⅛ teaspoon pepper
- ½ cup cream-style cottage cheese
- 4 beaten eggs
- ¼ cup grated Parmesan cheese
- 1 tablespoon snipped parsley
- 1 tablespoon snipped chives
- 1 tablespoon all-purpose flour
- ⅛ teaspoon garlic powder
- 2 tablespoons cooking oil

For sauce, in a medium skillet melt butter or margarine; add chopped tomatoes, salt, basil, oregano, and pepper. Cover and simmer about 5 minutes or till tomatoes are softened. Uncover and cook for 5 minutes longer. Remove from heat; set aside.

Drain cottage cheese, discarding liquid; press curds through a sieve. Combine cottage cheese, beaten eggs, Parmesan cheese, snipped parsley, snipped chives, flour, and garlic powder; beat smooth with a rotary beater. In a skillet heat oil over medium-low heat. To make patties, drop a scant *1 tablespoon* of the egg mixture into the hot oil. (Mixture will be thin.) Cook 4 at a time, about 1 minute on each side. Remove from skillet; set aside. Repeat with remaining egg mixture. Add more oil, if necessary.

Add the egg pattles to the tomato sauce. Cover and simmer for 2 to 3 minutes or till the sauce and patties are heated through. Serve egg patties with tomato sauce. Makes 3 servings.

CASHEW-SPROUT OMELET

Provides 27% U.S. RDA of protein per serving —

- 2 teaspoons butter *or* margarine
- 2 teaspoons all-purpose flour
  Dash salt
- ½ cup milk
- ¼ cup shredded cheddar cheese
- 1 2½-ounce jar whole mushrooms, drained
- ¼ cup cashews
- 4 eggs
- ¼ cup chopped cashews
- 2 tablespoons water
- ⅛ teaspoon pepper
- 1 tablespoon butter *or* margarine
- ½ cup alfalfa sprouts

For cheese sauce, in a small saucepan melt the 2 teaspoons butter or margarine. Stir in flour and salt. Add milk all at once. Cook and stir till thickened and bubbly. Cook and stir 1 to 2 minutes more. Add cheese, stirring till melted. Stir in drained mushrooms and the ¼ cup cashews.

Using a fork, beat eggs, ¼ cup chopped cashews, water, and pepper till well blended but not frothy. In an 8-inch skillet with flared sides, heat the 1 tablespoon butter or margarine till it sizzles and browns slightly. Lift and tilt the pan to coat sides. Add egg mixture; cook over medium heat. As eggs set, run a spatula around edge of skillet, lifting the eggs to allow the uncooked portion to flow underneath. When eggs are set but still shiny, remove from heat.

Spoon *half* of the cheese sauce across center of omelet. Top with *half* of the alfalfa sprouts. Lift ⅓ of the cooked omelet and fold over the filling in the center. Fold the remaining ⅓ of the omelet over all. Slide omelet onto a warmed platter. Top with remaining cheese sauce and alfalfa sprouts. Makes 3 servings.

42

Fried Rice Patties with Peanut Sauce
(See recipe, page 26)

CARROT-CAULIFLOWER PASTA TOSS

Pictured on pages 30 and 31
Provides 28% U.S. RDA of protein per serving—

  2 medium carrots, cut into julienne strips (1 cup)
  1 cup fresh cauliflower flowerets or ½ of a 10-ounce package frozen cauliflower
  1 cup frozen peas (½ of a 10-ounce package)
  ¼ cup sliced green onion
  1 clove garlic, minced
  2 tablespoons butter *or* margarine
  2 tablespoons all-purpose flour
  ¼ teaspoon salt
  ¼ teaspoon dry mustard
  ⅛ teaspoon pepper
1 ¼ cups milk
  1 cup shredded fontina *or* Gruyère cheese (4 ounces)
  ⅓ cup dairy sour cream
  2 tablespoons dry white wine
  8 ounces spaghetti, linguine, *or* other pasta, cooked (4 cups)
  2 tablespoons butter *or* margarine
  ¼ cup sliced almonds, toasted

Cook carrot strips, cauliflower, and peas in boiling salted water about 8 minutes or till vegetables are crisp-tender. Drain and set aside.

Meanwhile, to prepare the vegetable sauce, cook green onion and garlic in 2 tablespoons butter till onion is tender but not brown. Stir in flour, salt, mustard, and pepper. Add milk all at once. Cook and stir till thickened and bubbly. Cook and stir 1 to 2 minutes more. Remove from heat. Add cheese, stirring till melted. Stir in sour cream, wine, and cooked vegetables. Heat through; *do not boil.*

Toss hot cooked pasta with 2 tablespoons butter or margarine and the vegetable sauce. Top with sliced, toasted almonds. Makes 4 servings.

CALIFORNIA VEGETABLE PLATTER

Provides 34% U.S. RDA of protein per serving—

  2 cups sliced fresh mushrooms
  1 small red *or* green sweet pepper, cut into strips
  1 clove garlic, minced
  1 tablespoon butter *or* margarine
  1 cup fresh pea pods *or* one 6-ounce package frozen pea pods, thawed
  2 tablespoons butter *or* margarine
  2 tablespoons all-purpose flour
  1 teaspoon dried basil, crushed
  ½ teaspoon salt
1 ¼ cups light cream *or* milk
  2 cups cream-style cottage cheese *or* ricotta cheese, drained
  ¼ cup grated Parmesan cheese
  ¼ cup pine nuts *or* coarsely chopped walnuts
12 ounces fettucine *or* other pasta, cooked (6 cups)
  2 tablespoons butter *or* margarine

In a saucepan cook mushrooms, red or green sweet pepper strips, and minced garlic in the 1 tablespoon butter till tender. Add pea pods; cook 2 minutes or till pea pods are crisp-tender. Set aside.

Meanwhile, prepare vegetable sauce. In a medium saucepan melt 2 tablespoons butter or margarine. Stir in flour, basil, and salt. Add cream or milk all at once; cook and stir till thickened and bubbly. Cook and stir 1 to 2 minutes more. Remove from heat; stir in cottage or ricotta cheese and Parmesan cheese. Place sauce in a blender or food processor container. Cover; blend or process till smooth. Return to saucepan; stir in mushroom mixture and the nuts. Heat through; *do not boil.*

Toss hot pasta with 2 tablespoons butter and vegetable sauce. Serves 6.

MEDITERRANEAN STROGANOFF

Provides 26% U.S. RDA of protein per serving—

**2 cups cauliflower flowerets *or*
    one 10-ounce package frozen
    cauliflower**
**1½ cups fresh broccoli cut into
    bite-size pieces *or* one
    10-ounce package frozen cut
    broccoli**
1½ cups thinly bias-sliced carrots
3 tablespoons butter *or* margarine
3 cups sliced fresh mushrooms
1 small onion, sliced
1 clove garlic, minced
2 tablespoons all-purpose flour
2 cups light cream *or* milk
**½ teaspoon instant chicken
    bouillon granules**
⅓ cup sliced pitted ripe olives
1 cup ricotta cheese
¾ cup dairy sour cream
½ cup grated Parmesan cheese
**12 ounces linguine *or* other pasta,
    cooked (6 cups)**
2 tablespoons butter *or* margarine

In a large saucepan cook cauliflower, broccoli, and carrots, covered, in boiling salted water about 5 minutes or till crisp-tender; drain. Cut up any large pieces of cauliflower. Set vegetables aside.

Meanwhile, prepare sauce. In a Dutch oven or saucepan melt the 3 tablespoons butter or margarine; add the sliced mushrooms, sliced onion, and minced garlic. Cook over medium-high heat for 5 to 7 minutes or till onions are tender but not brown, stirring occasionally.

Stir flour into mushroom mixture. Add cream or milk and chicken bouillon granules all at once; cook and stir till thickened and bubbly. Cook and stir 1 to 2 minutes more. Stir in the drained broccoli mixture and olives. Heat through.

In a small bowl combine the ricotta cheese, sour cream, and *half* of the Parmesan cheese. Gradually stir about *1 cup* of the hot vegetable mixture into the sour cream mixture; return all of the sour cream mixture to the saucepan. Cook over medium heat for 3 to 4 minutes or till heated through; *do not boil.* Toss hot pasta with the 2 tablespoons butter and the vegetable sauce. Sprinkle with the remaining Parmesan cheese. Makes 6 servings.

VEGETABLE WELSH RABBIT

Provides 29% U.S. RDA of protein per serving—

**1 10-ounce package frozen cut
    broccoli**
¼ cup chopped onion
2 tablespoons butter *or* margarine
3 tablespoons all-purpose flour
½ teaspoon dry mustard
¼ teaspoon salt
⅛ teaspoon ground red pepper
1½ cups milk
1½ teaspoons Worcestershire sauce
**2 cups shredded cheddar cheese
    (8 ounces)**
**1 8-ounce can water chestnuts,
    drained and sliced**
**12 slices bread, toasted and
    quartered**

Cook broccoli according to package directions; drain well. In a medium saucepan cook chopped onion in butter or margarine till tender but not brown. Stir in flour, dry mustard, salt, and ground red pepper. Add milk and Worcestershire sauce all at once. Cook and stir till thickened and bubbly. Cook and stir 1 to 2 minutes more.

Add shredded cheese, stirring till melted. Add cooked broccoli and water chestnuts. Spoon the cheese mixture over the toasted bread. Makes 6 servings.

Pasta Primavera

PASTA PRIMAVERA

Provides 27% U.S. RDA of protein per serving—

- 3 tablespoons butter *or* margarine
- 1 8-ounce package frozen cut asparagus, thawed
- 2 medium carrots, very thinly bias-sliced (1 cup)
- ½ cup chopped onion
- 1 clove garlic, minced
- 1 teaspoon dried thyme, crushed
- 1 6-ounce package frozen pea pods, thawed
- 1 cup cashews
- ¼ cup dry white wine
- 6 ounces linguine *or* other pasta, cooked (3 cups)
- ⅓ cup grated Parmesan cheese

Melt butter in a 10-inch skillet. Stir in asparagus, carrots, onion, garlic, thyme, ¼ teaspoon *salt*, and ¼ teaspoon *pepper*. Cook about 8 minutes or till asparagus is crisp-tender. Add pea pods, cashews, and wine. Cook 1 to 2 minutes longer or till all vegetables are crisp-tender. Toss hot pasta with vegetables and Parmesan cheese. Makes 4 servings.

BEER-CHEESE NOODLES

Provides 35% U.S. RDA of protein per serving—

- 3 medium carrots, thinly sliced
- 1 10-ounce package frozen cut broccoli
- 3 tablespoons butter *or* margarine
- ¼ cup all-purpose flour
- ½ teaspoon salt
- ⅛ teaspoon pepper
- 1 cup milk
- 1 cup shredded Swiss cheese
- 1 cup shredded Monterey Jack cheese
- ¾ cup beer
- 6 ounces green noodles *or* spaghetti, cooked (4½ cups)
- 2 tablespoons butter *or* margarine

Cook carrots and broccoli, covered, in a small amount of boiling salted water for 8 minutes or till just tender. Drain; set aside.

Meanwhile, prepare vegetable sauce. In a saucepan melt the 3 tablespoons butter or margarine; stir in flour, salt, and pepper. Add milk all at once. Cook and stir over medium heat till mixture is thickened and bubbly. Cook and stir 1 to 2 minutes more. Add Swiss and Monterey Jack cheeses and beer, stirring till cheeses are melted. Stir in cooked carrots and broccoli. Toss hot cooked pasta with the 2 tablespoons butter and the vegetable sauce. Makes 4 servings.

GARBANZO-SAUCED SPAGHETTI

Provides 31% U.S. RDA of protein per serving—

- 1 16-ounce can tomatoes, cut up
- 1 6-ounce can tomato paste
- 1 medium onion, chopped (½ cup)
- 1 tablespoon instant beef bouillon granules
- 1 teaspoon sugar
- 1 teaspoon dried oregano, crushed
- ½ teaspoon dried basil, crushed
- ⅛ teaspoon pepper
- 1½ cups water
- 2 15-ounce cans garbanzo *or* navy beans, drained
- 1 cup shredded American cheese
- ¼ cup snipped parsley
- 12 ounces spaghetti *or* other pasta, cooked (6 cups)

In a 3-quart saucepan combine *undrained* tomatoes, tomato paste, onion, bouillon granules, sugar, oregano, basil, and pepper; stir in water. Simmer, uncovered, 30 minutes or to the desired consistency. Add beans and cheese, stirring till cheese is melted. Stir in parsley. Serve over hot spaghetti. Pass grated Parmesan cheese, if desired. Makes 8 servings.

47

GRUYÈRE CHEESE SOUP

Provides 34% U.S. RDA of protein per serving—

- **1 pound fresh broccoli *or* one 10-ounce package frozen cut broccoli, thawed**
- **½ cup water**
- **1½ teaspoons instant chicken bouillon granules**
- **2 medium carrots, thinly bias-sliced**

● ● ●

- **¼ cup sliced green onion**
- **3 tablespoons butter *or* margarine**
- **3 tablespoons all-purpose flour**
- **½ teaspoon ground nutmeg**
- **¼ teaspoon white pepper**
- **3 cups milk**
- **2 cups shredded Monterey Jack cheese (8 ounces)**
- **1 cup shredded Gruyère cheese (4 ounces)**
- **¼ cup dry sherry**

If using fresh broccoli, wash and remove outer leaves and tough parts of stalks. Cut stalks into small bite-size pieces, about ¾ x ½-inch (about 4 cups).

In a saucepan heat water and chicken bouillon granules. Place carrots in the saucepan; top with fresh or thawed broccoli pieces. Cook, tightly covered, about 10 minutes or till vegetables are crisp-tender. Drain, reserving liquid.

Meanwhile, in a saucepan cook green onion in butter or margarine till tender but not brown. Stir in flour, ground nutmeg, and white pepper. If necessary, add enough water to reserved vegetable liquid to make ½ cup. Add liquid and milk to green onion mixture all at once. Cook and stir till thickened and bubbly. Cook and stir 1 to 2 minutes more. Add shredded Monterey Jack cheese and shredded Gruyère cheese, stirring till cheeses are melted. Stir in cooked vegetables and sherry. Heat through. Makes 6 servings.

HERBED LENTIL-VEGETABLE STEW

Provides 36% U.S. RDA of protein per serving—

- **1½ cups dry lentils**
- **4 cups water**
- **1 16-ounce can tomatoes, cut up**
- **1 medium onion, chopped (½ cup)**
- **1 small green pepper, chopped (½ cup)**
- **1 stalk celery, chopped (½ cup)**
- **1 tablespoon Worcestershire sauce**
- **2 teaspoons salt**
- **1½ teaspoons dried thyme, crushed**
- **1 teaspoon dried oregano, crushed Few drops bottled hot pepper sauce**
- **2 medium carrots, chopped (1 cup)**
- **⅔ cup water**
- **⅓ cup bulgur wheat Dash salt**
- **1½ cups shredded cheddar cheese (6 ounces)**
- **6 tablespoons shelled sunflower seed**

Rinse lentils. In a saucepan combine lentils, the 4 cups water, *undrained* tomatoes, the onion, green pepper, celery, Worcestershire sauce, 2 teaspoons salt, thyme, oregano, and hot pepper sauce. Bring mixture to boiling; reduce heat. Cover and simmer for 30 minutes, stirring occasionally. Stir carrots into the lentil mixture. Bring to boiling, stirring constantly. Reduce heat and simmer, covered, about 30 minutes more, stirring occasionally. Using the back of a spoon, slightly mash the lentils. Meanwhile, combine remaining water with bulgur and dash salt. Bring to boiling; reduce heat and cover. Simmer for 15 minutes. To serve, mound some of the bulgur on each portion of lentil stew. Sprinkle each serving with ¼ *cup* of the cheese and *1 tablespoon* of the sunflower seed. Makes 6 servings.

48

HEARTY BEAN STEW

Provides 30% U.S. RDA of protein per serving—

- 2 15½-ounce cans red kidney beans
- 1 15-ounce can garbanzo beans
- 2 medium potatoes, peeled, quartered lengthwise, and sliced
- 1 cup thinly sliced carrot
- ½ cup chopped onion
- 1 6-ounce can tomato paste
- 2 teaspoons chili powder
- 1 teaspoon dried basil, crushed
- ¼ teaspoon garlic powder
- ¼ teaspoon pepper
- 8 ounces Monterey Jack cheese, cut into ½-inch cubes (2 cups)

In a Dutch oven combine all ingredients *except* cheese with 2½ cups *water* and 1 teaspoon *salt*. Bring to boiling; reduce heat. Cover; simmer 30 minutes or till vegetables are tender. Top *each* serving with ⅓ *cup* cheese cubes. Serves 6.

BARLEY-CHEESE SOUP

Pictured on page 28

Provides 25% U.S. RDA of protein per serving—

- ½ cup quick-cooking barley
- ¼ cup chopped onion
- 2 tablespoons butter *or* margarine
- 2 tablespoons all-purpose flour
- 1 teaspoon instant beef bouillon granules
- 1½ cups milk
- ¾ cup shredded American cheese
- ¾ cup shredded cheddar cheese
- ⅓ cup beer
- 2 tablespoons snipped parsley
- ¼ cup croutons (optional)

Cook barley according to package directions. Drain and set aside. Meanwhile, cook onion in butter till tender. Stir in flour, bouillon granules, and ⅛ teaspoon *pepper*. Add milk and ½ cup *water* all at once. Cook and stir till thickened and bubbly. Cook and stir 1 to 2 minutes more. Add cooked barley, cheeses, and beer, stirring till cheeses are melted. Before serving, stir in parsley. Top with croutons, if desired. Makes 4 servings.

MINESTRONE

Provides 26% U.S. RDA of protein per serving—

- 1 cup dry navy beans
- 1 28-ounce can tomatoes, cut up
- 2 medium carrots, cut into 2-inch sticks
- 2 stalks celery, bias-sliced
- 1 10½-ounce can condensed beef broth
- ½ cup chopped onion
- 1 clove garlic, minced
- 2 teaspoons dried basil, crushed
- 2 large bay leaves
- 1 teaspoon sugar
- 1 teaspoon dried thyme, crushed
- 4 ounces spaghetti, broken into 2-inch lengths
- 2 medium zucchini, thinly sliced
- ⅓ cup grated Parmesan cheese

Rinse beans. In a Dutch oven or kettle combine beans and 9 cups *water*. Bring to boiling; reduce heat and simmer 2 minutes. Remove from heat. Cover; let stand 1 hour. Stir 1 teaspoon *salt* into beans and soaking water. Bring to boiling; reduce heat. Cover and simmer for 45 minutes to 1 hour or till beans are tender. Drain, reserving 4 cups liquid. To beans add *undrained* tomatoes, carrots, celery, beef broth, onion, garlic, basil, bay leaves, sugar, thyme, and reserved bean liquid. Bring to boiling. Stir in spaghetti. Reduce heat; cover and simmer about 20 minutes. Add zucchini; cover and simmer about 10 minutes or till vegetables are tender and spaghetti is tender yet firm. Remove bay leaves. Sprinkle *each* serving with about *1 tablespoon* of Parmesan cheese. Serves 6.

49

Spicy Vegetable Chili

MACARONI-BEAN STEW

Provides 32% U.S. RDA of protein per serving—

1 15½-ounce can red kidney
    beans, drained
1 8-ounce can tomato sauce
1 cup water
½ cup corkscrew macaroni
¼ cup dry red wine
1 medium carrot, sliced
1 2-ounce can mushroom stems and
    pieces
2 tablespoons chopped onion
2 tablespoons sliced pimiento-
    stuffed olives
½ teaspoon sugar
½ teaspoon dried basil, crushed
¼ cup grated Parmesan cheese

In a saucepan combine kidney beans, tomato sauce, water, macaroni, wine, carrot, *undrained* mushrooms, onion, olives, sugar, and basil. Cover and simmer about 30 minutes or till carrot and macaroni are tender. Ladle into soup bowls. Sprinkle with Parmesan cheese. Makes 2 servings.

BROCCOLI-TOFU SOUP

Provides 28% U.S. RDA of protein per serving—

8 ounces fresh tofu (bean curd)
1 tablespoon minced dried onion
½ teaspoon instant chicken
    bouillon granules
¼ teaspoon dried basil, crushed
1 10-ounce package frozen
    chopped broccoli
1 10¾-ounce can condensed
    cream of potato soup
2 cups milk
¾ cup shredded Swiss cheese

Place tofu in a double thickness of cheesecloth or paper toweling. Press gently to extract as much moisture as possible. Cut tofu into ½-inch cubes. In a saucepan combine dried onion, bouillon granules, basil, and ½ cup *water*. Bring to boiling. Stir in frozen broccoli; return to boiling. Reduce heat; cover and simmer 5 minutes or till tender. *Do not drain.* Stir in soup. Gradually add milk; bring to boiling. Reduce heat. Add tofu and cheese, stirring till cheese is melted. Makes 4 servings.

SPICY VEGETABLE CHILI

Provides 38% U.S. RDA of protein per serving—

3 medium onions, sliced (1½ cups)
3 stalks celery, sliced (1½ cups)
2 green peppers, sliced (1½ cups)
4 cloves garlic, minced
2 tablespoons olive oil
2 28-ounce cans tomatoes, cut up
3 15½-ounce cans red kidney beans
1 15-ounce can great northern
    beans *or* navy beans
1 cup beer *or* water
½ cup raisins
½ cup cashews
¼ cup vinegar
1 tablespoon chili powder
1 tablespoon snipped parsley
2 teaspoons salt
1 bay leaf
1½ teaspoons dried basil, crushed
1½ teaspoons dried oregano,
    crushed
½ teaspoon pepper
¼ teaspoon bottled hot pepper
    sauce
2 cups shredded cheddar cheese

Cook onion, celery, green pepper, and garlic in oil till tender. Stir in *undrained* tomatoes, *undrained* kidney and great northern beans, along with all remaining ingredients *except* cheese. Bring to boiling; reduce heat. Cover and simmer for 1 hour. Remove cover; simmer 1 hour longer. Remove bay leaf. Top *each* serving with ¼ *cup* of shredded cheese. Serves 8.

MANDARIN VEGETABLE PANCAKES

Provides 31% U.S. RDA of protein per serving —

  1½ **cups all-purpose flour**
  ¼ **teaspoon salt**
  2 **tablespoons all-purpose flour**
      Cooking oil
  1 **cup thinly sliced broccoli**
  2 **carrots, cut into julienne**
        strips
  2 **tablespoons cooking oil**
  1 **cup chopped green pepper**
  ⅔ **cup slivered almonds, toasted**
  ½ **cup sliced zucchini**
  3 **tablespoons soy sauce**
  2 **tablespoons dry sherry**
  5 **beaten eggs**

For pancakes, stir together the 1½ cups flour and salt. Pour ½ cup *boiling water* slowly into flour. Stir till combined. Stir in 3 tablespoons *cold water*. When dough is cool enough to handle, knead in the 2 tablespoons all-purpose flour till smooth and elastic (8 to 10 minutes).

Shape dough into a ball. Place the dough in a bowl; cover with a damp towel. Let stand 15 to 20 minutes.

Turn dough onto a lightly floured surface. Form into a 12-inch-long roll. Cut roll into 1-inch pieces. Flatten each piece of dough with the palm of your hand. Roll each piece into a 6-inch circle. Brush the surface of *one* side of each pancake lightly with oil.

Stack two pancakes with greased sides together. In a heavy ungreased skillet or griddle cook the pancake stacks, a few at a time, over medium heat 20 to 30 seconds on each side or till bubbles appear on surface of pancake (a few golden spots will appear.) Quickly remove pancakes from pan and gently separate the paired pancakes. Place all the pancakes on a baking sheet; cover with a dry towel to keep

moist. Repeat cooking and covering with remaining pancakes.

In a covered saucepan cook broccoli and carrots in boiling salted water for 5 minutes; drain well. Preheat a wok or large skillet over high heat; add the 2 tablespoons oil. Stir-fry broccoli, carrots, green pepper, almonds, and zucchini 2 to 3 minutes or till vegetables are crisp-tender. Add soy sauce and sherry. Add beaten eggs to the mixture; reduce heat to low. Cook eggs about 5 minutes or till cooked through but still shiny. (Don't stir eggs till the mixture starts to set at the bottom. Avoid breaking up the eggs more than necessary.) Place a scant ½ cup egg mixture off center on the unbrowned side of *each* pancake. Starting at edge, roll pancake. Keep warm while rolling remaining pancakes. Serve immediately. Makes 4 servings.

EGG BURRITOS

Provides 34% U.S. RDA of protein per serving —

  6 **10-inch flour tortillas**
  6 **eggs**
  2 **tablespoons butter *or***
      margarine
  ⅓ **cup mild green chili salsa**
  1½ **cups bean sprouts *or* alfalfa**
        sprouts
  1 **medium tomato, chopped**
  1 **avocado, seeded, peeled, and**
      chopped

Wrap tortillas tightly in foil; heat in a 350° oven for 5 to 10 minutes or till heated through. In a skillet fry eggs in butter or margarine. Place one egg atop each tortilla. Top *each* with about *1 tablespoon* of the salsa, ¼ *cup* of the bean or alfalfa sprouts, and *some* of the tomato and avocado. Fold sides of tortilla so they overlap atop mixture. Fold remaining edges toward center to form a square packet. Serve warm. Makes 3 servings.

52

CHEESY CORN AND EGG TACOS

Provides 35% U.S. RDA of protein per serving—

- 8 taco shells
- 6 eggs
- 1 cup frozen whole kernel corn, cooked and drained, *or* 1 cup canned whole kernel corn, drained
- 1 cup shredded American, cheddar, *or* Monterey Jack cheese
- 1 4-ounce can green chili peppers, rinsed, seeded, and chopped
- ¼ teaspoon salt
- ⅛ teaspoon pepper
- ¼ cup chopped onion
- 1 tablespoon butter *or* margarine
- 2 cups shredded lettuce
- 1 large tomato, chopped
  Bottled taco sauce (optional)

Arrange taco shells on a baking sheet lined with paper toweling. Warm in a 250° oven while preparing egg mixture. In a mixing bowl beat eggs. Stir in drained frozen or canned corn, shredded American cheese, cheddar cheese, or Monterey Jack cheese, chopped green chili peppers, salt, and pepper; mix well.

Cook the onion in butter or margarine till tender but not brown. Pour the egg-corn mixture over the hot onion in the skillet. Cook over low heat, without stirring, till the egg mixture begins to set on the bottom and around the edges.

Lift and fold the partially cooked eggs so the uncooked portion flows underneath. Continue lifting and folding the eggs about 5 minutes or till they are cooked through but are still shiny. Remove from heat immediately.

Spoon about ¼ *cup* of the egg mixture into each taco shell. Top each taco with some lettuce and chopped tomato. Pass bottled taco sauce, if desired. Serves 4.

SMOKY RED BEANS

Provides 33% U.S. RDA of protein per serving—

- 1 pound dry red beans
- 8 cups water
- ½ teaspoon salt
- 1 cup sliced celery
- 2 small onions, cut into wedges
- 1 green pepper, cut into ½-inch pieces
- 1 clove garlic, minced
- 2 tablespoons butter *or* margarine
- ½ cup beer (optional)
- 1 6-ounce can tomato paste
- ¼ cup bottled hot-style barbecue sauce
- 1 tablespoon brown sugar
- 1 tablespoon Worcestershire sauce
- 2 teaspoons vinegar
- 2 teaspoons prepared mustard
- ¼ teaspoon salt
- ¼ teaspoon pepper
- 1 cup corn chips
- ½ cup shredded smoky cheddar cheese

Rinse beans; combine beans and water. Bring to boiling; reduce heat and simmer 2 minutes. Remove from heat. Cover; let stand 1 hour. Stir the ½ teaspoon salt into beans and soaking water. Bring to boiling; reduce heat. Cover and simmer about 1 hour or till beans are tender. Drain, reserving cooking liquid.

In a Dutch oven cook sliced celery, onion wedges, green pepper pieces, and garlic in butter or margarine till tender but not brown. Stir in beans, 2½ cups reserved cooking liquid, beer, if desired (if not using beer, add ½ cup more cooking liquid), tomato paste, barbecue sauce, brown sugar, Worcestershire sauce, vinegar, mustard, the ¼ teaspoon salt, and pepper. Bring to boiling; reduce heat. Simmer, uncovered, for 20 minutes. Serve in individual bowls. Top with the corn chips and cheese. Makes 6 servings.

PASTA · & · RICE

Corkscrew Noodles

Elbow Macaroni

Fettucine

Lasagna

According to Italians, pasta should be cooked to a stage called *al dente* (to the tooth), which means that the pasta should be tender but still slightly firm. It's not hard to achieve this doneness— just follow the cooking instructions given here and the cooking times given with the pasta descriptions.

When cooking pasta, it's important to use a sufficiently large kettle or Dutch oven. For every 8 ounces of pasta that you intend to cook, put 3 quarts of water and 1 tablespoon of salt into the kettle. If desired, you also can add 1 tablespoon of cooking oil to help keep large pasta separated.

Bring the water mixture to a rolling boil and add the pasta a little at a time so the water does not stop boiling. (Hold long pasta, such as spaghetti, at one end and dip the other end into the water. As the pasta softens, gently curl it around in the kettle till all of it is immersed.) Slightly reduce the heat and continue boiling the pasta, uncovered, till it is tender but still slightly firm. (See the cooking times given with the pasta descriptions.) Stir occasionally to prevent the pasta from sticking. Frequently taste the pasta near the end of the cooking time to test it for doneness.

To serve hot pasta, immediately drain it in a colander. *Do not rinse.* Transfer to a warm serving dish and serve immediately.

Linguine

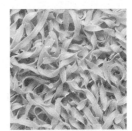

Manicotti

Medium Noodles

Medium Shells

To serve cold pasta, such as in a salad, drain the cooked pasta in a colander. *Rinse* with cold water and drain again.

You can keep hot pasta warm for a short time by returning it to the kettle. Add 2 to 3 tablespoons of butter and cover the kettle to keep warm. Eight ounces of uncooked pasta will make about 4 cups of cooked pasta.

Corkscrew noodles are twisted macaroni. They add interest to casseroles and salads. Cook for about 12 minutes.

Elbow macaroni is often an ingredient in casseroles, main dishes, and salads. Cook it for about 10 minutes.

Fettucine are flat pasta strands that may be straight or curled. Fettucine is used in casseroles and with sauce. Cook for 10 to 12 minutes.

Lasagna noodles are flat and about 1½ to 2 inches wide. The edges may be straight or ruffled. They are usually used in casseroles. Cook for 10 to 12 minutes.

Linguine are narrow flat strands of pasta. Use linguine in casseroles or with a sauce. Cook for 8 to 10 minutes.

Manicotti are large tube-shaped pasta about 4 inches long, with diagonally cut ends. They are usually filled. Cook for about 18 minutes.

Medium noodles are thin, flat strips of pasta about 2 inches long. Fine (narrow) noodles and wide noodles also are available. Use them in casseroles and soups.

Mostaccioli

Ravioli

Rigatoni

Spaghetti

Cook medium noodles for about 10 minutes.

Medium shells resemble a conch shell in shape. Small or jumbo shells also are available. They can be stuffed or used in casseroles. Cook the medium shells for about 15 minutes.

Mostaccioli are large macaroni about 2 inches long that may have ridged or plain surfaces. The ends are always cut diagonally. Use mostaccioli in casseroles and main dishes. Cook for about 14 minutes.

Ravioli are small pasta squares with pinked or notched edges. They usually are stuffed and served with a sauce. They also can be fried. Cook for 6 to 8 minutes.

Rigatoni is a grooved macaroni with a shape like manicotti but smaller and with ends cut straight. Use rigatoni in casseroles, side dishes, and main dishes. Cook for about 15 minutes.

Spaghetti is a very familiar form of long, thin pasta used in casseroles or served with a sauce. Cook spaghetti for 10 to 12 minutes.

Since there are several types of rice available in the supermarket, buying and using the right type for a particular recipe can be confusing. One important rule to remember when you're using any type of rice is: Never wash it! Rice purchased in a sealed package does not need to be washed. It has already been washed, cleaned, and packaged under

Brown Rice

Long Grain Rice

Quick-Cooking Rice

Wild Rice

strict sanitary conditions. If you wash the rice again, you'll sacrifice water-soluble vitamins and minerals.

Also, cook the rice in the proper amount of water. Using too little water will not allow the rice to become done; using too much water will cause some loss of the water-soluble vitamins and minerals.

Brown rice is long grain rice that has had only the outer hull removed in processing. Since little is removed, brown rice retains many of its natural nutrients. It is slightly chewy and has a nutty flavor.

Long grain rice is long grain milled white rice. If properly cooked, the grains will remain separate and fluffy. White rice is also available in short and medium grains.

Quick-cooking rice has been specially developed to cook in a hurry. It is precooked and dehydrated before packaging. This process speeds your cooking time, but tends to make the rice stick together a bit more than long grain rice.

Wild rice isn't really rice at all. It belongs to a family of plants that grows in the marshes in Minnesota and Canada. Wild rice has a unique flavor and a chewy texture.

You can also buy several varieties of rice mixes. They are a combination of rice with dehydrated seasonings. Since rices vary in their cooking times, follow the package instructions.

OVEN

CHEESY GREEK PIE

Provides 27% U.S. RDA of protein per serving —

> 2   8-ounce packages cream cheese
> 2   eggs
> 2   cups shredded provolone cheese
> ½   cup cream-style cottage cheese
> ½   cup chopped ripe olives
> 1½ teaspoons garlic salt
> ½   cup butter *or* margarine, melted
> 9   17x13-inch sheets phyllo dough
> 2   10-ounce packages frozen
>   chopped spinach, cooked and
>   drained
> 1   beaten egg
>   Sliced pitted ripe olives

For filling, in a mixer bowl beat cream cheese on medium speed of electric mixer for 30 seconds. Add 2 eggs; beat till fluffy. Stir in shredded provolone cheese, cottage cheese, the ½ cup chopped olives, and garlic salt.

Brush the bottom of a 13x9x2-inch baking dish with some melted butter. Place *1 sheet* of phyllo in the bottom of the dish, allowing sides to overlap edges. Brush with melted butter. Repeat with phyllo and butter 5 times.

Spread filling over phyllo; top with spinach. Fold edges of phyllo over filling. Cut remaining sheets of phyllo in half crosswise; place on top of phyllo in dish, brushing butter between sheets. With a sharp knife, score *top layers* of phyllo in a diamond pattern. Bake in a 375° oven about 25 minutes. Brush with some of the beaten egg; bake 5 minutes more or till golden. Finish cutting. Let stand 10 minutes before serving. Garnish each serving with a sliced olive. Serves 9.

ARTICHOKE-MUSHROOM PIE

Provides 36% U.S. RDA of protein per serving —

> 2   9-inch frozen unbaked deep-dish
>   pastry shells
> 2   cloves garlic, minced
> 1   tablespoon cooking oil
> 1   14-ounce can artichoke hearts,
>   drained and halved
> 1   4-ounce can mushroom stems and
>   pieces, drained
> 4   beaten eggs
> 1   cup shredded mozzarella cheese
>   (4 ounces)
> 1   cup shredded Gruyère cheese
>   (4 ounces)
> 1   cup shredded cheddar cheese
>   (4 ounces)
> ¼   cup chopped ripe olives
> ⅛   teaspoon pepper

Remove pastry shells from freezer. Turn one pastry shell out of foil pan onto waxed paper; let thaw for 10 minutes. Press gently to flatten pastry shell.

In a small skillet cook garlic in hot oil; stir in artichokes and mushrooms. Spoon artichoke mixture onto the bottom of the pastry shell in the pan. In a bowl combine beaten eggs, mozzarella cheese, Gruyère cheese, cheddar cheese, chopped olives, and pepper; pour over artichoke mixture. Place flattened pastry shell atop cheese mixture; turn under and crimp the edges. Cut slits in top to allow for escape of steam. Preheat a baking sheet in a 350° oven. Bake the pie on the baking sheet in the 350° oven for 40 to 50 minutes. Let stand for 10 minutes before serving. Serves 6.

VEGETABLE PIE

Provides 29% U.S. RDA of protein per serving—

 1 cup all-purpose flour
 1 cup whole wheat flour
 1/4 cup finely chopped shelled
    sunflower seed
 1/4 teaspoon salt
 2/3 cup shortening *or* lard
 1 cup chopped zucchini
 1 cup chopped celery
 1/2 cup shredded carrot
 1/2 cup sliced fresh mushrooms
 1/2 cup chopped green pepper
 1 clove garlic, minced
 1 8-ounce can tomato sauce
 1 cup cut green beans, cooked
 1 tablespoon brown sugar
 1 teaspoon dried oregano, crushed
 1 teaspoon chili powder
 1/2 teaspoon dried basil, crushed
 2 cups shredded cheddar cheese
 1 tablespoon all-purpose flour
 1 beaten egg

Stir together the 1 cup all-purpose flour, whole wheat flour, sunflower seed, and salt. Cut in shortening or lard till pieces are the size of small peas. Sprinkle 1 tablespoon cold *water* over part of the mixture; gently toss with a fork. Push to side of bowl. Repeat, using 4 to 6 more tablespoons cold *water,* till all is moistened. Form dough into two balls. Roll *half* of the pastry to 1/8-inch thickness. Fit into a 9-inch pie plate. Trim. Cook zucchini, celery, carrot, mushrooms, green pepper, and garlic in 1/2 cup *water* just till tender; drain. Add tomato sauce, green beans, brown sugar, oregano, chili powder, basil, 1/2 teaspoon *salt,* and 1/4 teaspoon *pepper.* Simmer, uncovered, for 2 to 3 minutes. Toss cheese with the 1 tablespoon all-purpose flour; stir into vegetable mixture. Turn into pastry-lined pie plate.

Roll out remaining pastry; place atop vegetable mixture. Seal; crimp edges. Cut slits in top. Combine the egg and 1 tablespoon *water.* Brush over crust. Cover edge of piecrust with foil.

Bake in a 350° oven for 20 minutes. Remove foil; continue baking for 40 minutes or till golden. Let stand 10 minutes before serving. Serves 6.

HERBED PIE

Provides 28% U.S. RDA of protein per serving—

 1 1/2 cups herb-seasoned croutons *or*
    stuffing mix, finely crushed
 1/4 cup chopped almonds, toasted
 3 tablespoons butter *or* margarine,
    melted
 1 cup chopped onion
 1 clove garlic, minced
 2 tablespoons butter *or* margarine
 1/2 teaspoon dried savory, crushed
 1/2 teaspoon dried oregano, crushed
 3 cups sliced cauliflower
 1/2 cup sliced carrot
 2 cups shredded cheddar cheese
 3 eggs
 1/3 cup milk
 1/4 cup chopped almonds, toasted

Combine crushed croutons, 1/4 cup almonds, and the 3 tablespoons melted butter. Press mixture onto the bottom of a 9-inch pie plate. Bake in a 375° oven for 8 to 10 minutes or till golden; set aside.

Cook onion and garlic in the 2 tablespoons butter till tender. Add savory, oregano, 1/4 teaspoon *salt,* and dash *pepper;* mix well. Add cauliflower and carrot. Cover; simmer 8 to 10 minutes over low heat or till vegetables are crisp-tender. Sprinkle *half* of the cheese over crouton mixture; spoon vegetable mixture atop.

Beat together eggs and milk. Pour over vegetables. Bake in a 375° oven for 15 minutes. Top with remaining cheese and 1/4 cup almonds. Bake 10 to 15 minutes more or till cheese is melted. Let stand 10 minutes. Makes 6 servings.

57

Easy Cheesy Pie

THREE-VEGETABLE PIE

Provides 28% U.S. RDA of protein per serving—

3 **beaten eggs**
1½ **cups soft bread crumbs**
1½ **cups shredded cheddar cheese**
   (6 ounces)
½ **cup milk**
1½ **cups finely chopped carrots,**
   cooked and drained
1 **teaspoon dried basil, crushed**
1½ **cups finely chopped beets,**
   cooked and drained
1 **teaspoon dried tarragon, crushed**
1½ **cups finely chopped parsnips,**
   cooked and drained
   Pastry for Double-Crust Pie
½ **cup sliced pitted ripe olives**
1 **beaten egg**

Combine 3 eggs, bread crumbs, cheese, milk, 1 teaspoon *salt,* and ½ teaspoon *pepper.* Divide cheese mixture into thirds. To one third stir in carrots and basil. To another third stir in cooked beets and *half* of the tarragon. To the remaining third stir in parsnips and remaining tarragon. Set mixtures aside.

Prepare Pastry for Double-Crust Pie. Roll *half* of the pastry into a 14-inch circle. Line a 10-inch pie plate with pastry, allowing excess to hang over edge. Lightly score pastry into three sections. Spoon carrot mixture into one section, spoon the beet mixture into the second section, and spoon the parsnip mixture into the remaining section.

Place olives over the dividing lines between the mixtures. Roll out the remaining pastry into a 10 x 3-inch rectangle; cut lengthwise into twelve ¼ x 10-inch strips. Place strips atop filling in a lattice design; trim and flute edges. Brush pastry strips with the 1 beaten egg. Bake in a 375° oven for 30 to 40 minutes or till golden. Let the pie stand 10 minutes before serving. Makes 6 servings.

Pastry for Double-Crust Pie: Stir together 2 cups all-purpose *flour* and 1 teaspoon *salt.* Cut in ⅔ cup *shortening or lard* till pieces are the size of small peas. Sprinkle 1 tablespoon cold *water* over part of the mixture; toss with a fork. Push to side of bowl. Repeat, using 5 to 6 more tablespoons *water,* till all is moistened. Form dough into two balls.

EASY CHEESY PIE

Provides 27% U.S. RDA of protein per serving—

¼ **cup sliced green onion**
1 **tablespoon cooking oil**
1 **cup all-purpose flour**
1 **tablespoon baking powder**
½ **cup butter *or* margarine**
2 **beaten eggs**
¼ **cup milk**
2 **beaten eggs**
1½ **cups cream-style cottage cheese,**
   drained
1 **3-ounce package cream cheese,**
   softened
1 **tablespoon lemon juice**
2 **tablespoons bacon-flavored**
   vegetable protein chips
1 **tablespoon sesame seed, toasted**

Cook onion in oil till tender but not brown; set aside. Stir together flour, baking powder, and ½ teaspoon *salt.* Cut in butter till mixture resembles coarse crumbs. Stir in 2 beaten eggs, milk, and onion till nearly smooth. Spread *half* of the batter in an ungreased 9-inch pie plate. Set remaining batter aside.

For filling, beat together 2 beaten eggs, cottage cheese, cream cheese, and lemon juice; stir in vegetable protein chips. Pour filling over batter in pie plate. Spoon remaining batter atop. Top with sesame seed. Bake in a 325° oven for 45 minutes or till a knife inserted near center comes out clean. Let stand 10 minutes before serving. Makes 6 servings.

TOFU-LENTIL PIE

Provides 30% U.S. RDA of protein per serving—

Pastry for Single-Crust Pie
¾ cup dry lentils, cooked and
    drained (2 cups)
1 large green pepper, chopped
¼ cup tomato paste
1 teaspoon Worcestershire sauce
16 ounces fresh tofu (bean curd),
    drained and cut up
2 eggs
½ cup cream-style cottage cheese
¼ cup sliced green onion
1 tablespoon lightly packed fresh
    parsley (stems removed)
1 clove garlic

Prepare and roll out Pastry for Single-Crust Pie. Line a 9-inch quiche dish or pie plate with pastry. Trim to ½ inch beyond edge. Flute edge high. Bake in a 450° oven for 8 to 10 minutes; set aside.

Season cooked, drained lentils with *salt* and *pepper.* Add ⅓ *cup* of the chopped green pepper, tomato paste, and Worcestershire sauce. Spoon lentil mixture into the pastry-lined quiche dish or pie plate. In a blender container combine the tofu chunks, eggs, cottage cheese, green onion, parsley, garlic, ½ teaspoon *salt,* and dash *pepper;* cover and blend on low speed till smooth. Pour tofu mixture over lentil mixture in pastry-lined quiche dish or pie plate. Bake in a 325° oven for 30 minutes. Sprinkle with the remaining chopped green pepper. Let stand 10 minutes before serving. Makes 6 servings.

Pastry for Single-Crust Pie: Stir together 1 cup all-purpose *flour* and ½ teaspoon *salt;* cut in ⅓ cup *shortening or lard* till pieces are the size of small peas. Sprinkle 1 tablespoon cold *water* over part of the mixture; gently toss with a fork. Push to side of bowl. Repeat, using 2 to 3 more tablespoons *water,* till all is moistened. Form dough into a ball.

ZUCCHINI-CHEESE TURNOVERS

Provides 37% U.S. RDA of protein per serving—

1 cup cubed zucchini
¼ cup chopped onion
½ cup grated Parmesan cheese
½ cup shredded cheddar cheese
2 tablespoons all-purpose flour
¼ teaspoon dried thyme, crushed
¼ teaspoon dried marjoram,
    crushed
1 cup cream-style cottage cheese,
    drained
1 2-ounce can chopped mushrooms,
    drained
1 beaten egg
Whole Wheat Pastry
1 teaspoon sesame seed

Cook zucchini and onion in a small amount of water about 5 minutes or just till tender; drain well. Toss together Parmesan, cheddar cheese, flour, thyme, marjoram, and ¼ teaspoon *salt.* Stir zucchini, onion, cottage cheese, and mushrooms into cheese mixture. Stir 2 *tablespoons* of the egg into zucchini mixture.

Prepare Whole Wheat Pastry. Roll each half into a 9-inch circle. Place each circle on an ungreased baking sheet. Spoon *half* of the zucchini-cheese mixture over *half* of each circle; fold other half of each circle over. Moisten and seal edges. Brush tops with remaining beaten egg. Top with sesame seed. Cut slits in tops. Bake in a 400° oven for 25 to 30 minutes or till brown. Let stand 10 minutes. Serves 4.

Whole Wheat Pastry: Stir together ¾ cup all-purpose *flour,* ¾ cup *whole wheat flour,* and ¼ teaspoon *salt.* Cut in ⅓ cup *shortening* till pieces are the size of small peas. Sprinkle 1 tablespoon cold *water* over part of mixture; toss with a fork. Push to side of bowl. Repeat, using 4 more tablespoons *water.* Form into two balls.

MACARONI-CRUST PIZZA

Provides 34% U.S. RDA of protein per serving—

7 ounces elbow macaroni (2 cups)
2 beaten eggs
½ cup shredded Monterey Jack cheese (2 ounces)
¼ cup grated Parmesan cheese (1 ounce)
¼ cup milk
½ teaspoon dried basil, crushed
½ teaspoon dried oregano, crushed
⅛ teaspoon pepper
1 beaten egg
1 cup cream-style cottage cheese, drained
1 8-ounce can pizza sauce
¼ cup thinly sliced green onion
¼ cup finely chopped green pepper
¼ cup sliced pitted ripe olives
1 cup shredded Monterey Jack cheese (4 ounces)

To make crust, in a large saucepan cook macaroni according to package directions; drain well. In a mixing bowl combine the 2 beaten eggs, the ½ cup shredded Monterey Jack cheese, Parmesan cheese, milk, basil, oregano, and pepper. Add drained macaroni to egg and cheese mixture; mix well. Form macaroni mixture into a "crust" in a greased 10-inch pie plate or a greased 11-inch quiche dish. Bake in a 375° oven for 10 minutes.

For filling, in a bowl combine the 1 beaten egg and drained cottage cheese; pour on top of macaroni crust in pie plate or quiche dish. Pour pizza sauce over top of filling mixture; arrange green onion, chopped green pepper, and sliced ripe olives atop pizza sauce. Sprinkle with the 1 cup shredded Monterey Jack cheese. Return to 375° oven for 10 to 15 minutes more or till heated through. Let stand 10 minutes before serving. Makes 6 servings.

CHEESY EGG-VEGETABLE PIZZA

Provides 28% U.S. RDA of protein per serving—

1 package active dry yeast
½ cup warm water (110° to 115°)
1¾ cups packaged biscuit mix
1 7½-ounce can tomatoes, cut up
1 6-ounce can tomato paste
¼ cup water
¼ cup chopped onion
¾ teaspoon dried oregano, crushed
½ teaspoon garlic salt
½ teaspoon dried basil, crushed
  Dash bottled hot pepper sauce
5 sliced hard-cooked eggs
1 medium green pepper, cut into strips
1 4-ounce can sliced mushrooms, drained
1 cup shredded mozzarella cheese
½ cup shredded American cheese

For crust, soften yeast in warm water. Add biscuit mix to yeast; beat well. Turn dough out onto a pastry cloth that is well dusted with biscuit mix; knead dough 3 to 5 minutes. Cover; let rest 10 minutes. Pat or roll dough into a 13-inch circle; place on a greased 12-inch pizza pan. Build up edges of dough slightly. Bake in a 425° oven for 5 minutes.

Meanwhile, for topping, in a bowl combine *undrained* tomatoes, tomato paste, water, chopped onion, oregano, garlic salt, basil, and bottled hot pepper sauce. Arrange egg slices atop partially baked crust. Sprinkle egg slices lightly with salt. Arrange green pepper strips and drained mushrooms atop. Spoon tomato mixture over top and bake in a 425° oven for 15 minutes more.

Toss mozzarella cheese and American cheese together; sprinkle cheese mixture atop pizza. Bake about 5 minutes more or till cheese is melted. Makes 6 servings.

Wheat-Crust Pizza

WHEAT-CRUST PIZZA

Provides 27% U.S. RDA of protein per serving—

1 to 1¼ cups whole wheat flour
1 package active dry yeast
2 tablespoons grated Parmesan cheese
1 egg
2 teaspoons cooking oil
1 cup cream-style cottage cheese
1½ cups desired vegetables*
1½ cups shredded cheddar cheese
1 8-ounce can tomato sauce
1½ teaspoons Italian seasoning

Combine ½ *cup* of the flour, yeast, and Parmesan. Stir in ⅓ cup warm *water* (115° to 120°), egg, and oil. Beat at low speed of electric mixer for ½ minute, scraping bowl constantly. Beat 3 minutes at high speed. Stir in as much of the flour as you can mix in with a spoon. Turn onto a floured surface. Knead in enough remaining flour to make a moderately stiff dough that is smooth and elastic (about 5 minutes). Place dough in a greased bowl, turning once. Cover; let rise in a warm place till double (about 30 minutes). Punch down; pat or roll into a greased 12-inch pizza pan. Cover; let rise 20 to 30 minutes. Bake in a 425° oven for 5 minutes. Drain cottage cheese; spread atop hot crust. Arrange desired vegetables atop. Sprinkle ½ *cup* of the shredded cheese over top. Combine tomato sauce and seasoning; pour over cheese. Bake in a 425° oven for 15 minutes. Top with remaining cheese; return to oven. Bake 5 minutes more. Makes 4 servings.

*Note: For vegetables, choose any of the following—sliced mushrooms or water chestnuts; alfalfa or bean sprouts. *Precook till crisp-tender:* broccoli cuts; pea pods; sliced celery, carrots, red or green sweet pepper, or zucchini. *Precook till tender:* peeled, cubed winter or crookneck squash.

ALMOND QUICHE LORRAINE

Provides 31% U.S. RDA of protein per serving—

½ cup chopped onion
1 tablespoon butter *or* margarine
4 beaten eggs
1 cup light cream
1 cup milk
1 tablespoon all-purpose flour
½ teaspoon salt
Dash ground nutmeg
1½ cups shredded Swiss cheese (6 ounces)
1 cup sliced almonds, toasted
Pastry for Single-Crust Pie (see recipe, page 60)

In a small skillet cook the chopped onion in the butter or margarine till the onion is tender but not brown. In a bowl stir together the beaten eggs, light cream, milk, flour, salt, and nutmeg. Stir in the cooked onion, shredded Swiss cheese, and toasted sliced almonds; mix well. Set aside.

Prepare and roll out Pastry for Single-Crust Pie. Line a 9-inch quiche dish or pie plate with pastry; trim pastry to ½ inch beyond edge of quiche dish. Flute edge high. *Do not* prick crust. To keep crust in shape, line the unbaked pastry shell with a double thickness of heavy-duty foil. Fill with dried beans. Bake the pastry shell in a 450° oven for 5 minutes. Remove the heavy-duty foil and dried beans. Bake the pastry shell 5 to 7 minutes more or till the pastry is nearly done. Remove the pastry shell from the oven; reduce the oven temperature to 325°.

Pour the egg-cheese mixture into the *hot* pastry shell. If necessary, cover edges of pastry with foil to prevent overbrowning. Bake in a 325° oven for 40 to 45 minutes or till a knife inserted near center comes out clean. Let stand 10 minutes before serving. Makes 6 servings.

PUFFY CHEESE SOUFFLÉ

Provides 36% U.S. RDA of protein per serving—

    6 tablespoons butter *or* margarine
    ⅓ cup all-purpose flour
    ½ teaspoon salt
      Dash ground red pepper
    1½ cups milk
    3 cups shredded cheddar cheese
    6 egg yolks
    6 egg whites

Attach a foil collar to a 2-quart soufflé dish. To make the collar, measure enough foil to go around a 2-quart soufflé dish plus a 2- to 3-inch overlap. Fold foil into thirds lengthwise. Butter one side. Position foil around dish with buttered side in, letting collar extend 2 inches above top of dish; fasten with tape. Set aside.

In a saucepan melt the 6 tablespoons butter or margarine; stir in flour, salt, and ground red pepper. Add the milk all at once. Cook and stir till thickened and bubbly. Cook and stir 1 to 2 minutes more. Remove from heat. Add the cheese, stirring till melted. Beat egg yolks till thick and lemon colored. Slowly add the cheese mixture to the beaten egg yolks, stirring constantly. Cool slightly.

Using *clean* beaters, beat egg whites at medium speed of electric mixer about 2½ minutes or till stiff peaks form (tips stand straight). Gradually pour yolk mixture over beaten egg whites, folding to blend. Pour into the prepared ungreased 2-quart soufflé dish.

Bake in a 300° oven about 1½ hours or till a knife inserted near center comes out clean. *Do not* open oven door during baking. Test the soufflé at the end of suggested baking time while the soufflé is still in the oven. Gently peel off the foil collar; serve immediately, using two forks. Makes 6 servings.

BROCCOLI-CAMEMBERT SOUFFLÉ

Provides 25% U.S. RDA of protein per serving—

    1 10-ounce package frozen
      chopped broccoli
    ¼ cup butter *or* margarine
    ¼ cup all-purpose flour
    ½ teaspoon dried basil, crushed
    ¼ teaspoon salt
    1 cup milk
    5 ounces Camembert cheese, rind
      removed and cubed, *or*
      shredded Swiss cheese
    ½ cup grated Parmesan cheese
    5 egg yolks
    7 egg whites

To make a foil collar, measure enough foil to go around a 2-quart soufflé dish plus a 2- to 3-inch overlap. Fold foil into thirds lengthwise. Butter one side. Position foil around dish with buttered side in, letting collar extend 2 inches above top of dish; fasten with tape. Set aside. Cook broccoli according to package directions; drain well. Melt the ¼ cup butter. Stir in flour, basil, and salt. Add milk all at once; cook and stir till thickened and bubbly. Cook and stir 1 to 2 minutes more. Remove from heat. Add cheeses, stirring to melt. Stir in the drained broccoli.

Beat egg yolks till thick and lemon colored. Slowly add cheese mixture to egg yolks, stirring constantly. Cool slightly. Using *clean* beaters, beat egg whites till stiff peaks form. Gradually pour yolk mixture over beaten whites, folding to blend. Turn into prepared ungreased 2-quart soufflé dish. Bake in a 350° oven for 40 minutes or till a knife inserted near center comes out clean. *Do not* open oven door during baking. Test soufflé at the end of suggested baking time while soufflé is still in oven. Gently peel off collar; serve immediately. Serves 6.

64

BLUE CHEESE SOUFFLÉ

Provides 29% U.S. RDA of protein per serving—

- ¼ cup butter *or* margarine
- ⅓ cup all-purpose flour
- 1 teaspoon Worcestershire sauce
  Dash ground red pepper
- 1 cup milk
- 1 cup crumbled blue cheese
- 1 3-ounce package cream cheese, cut up and softened
- 4 eggs, separated

Melt butter. Stir in flour, Worcestershire, and red pepper. Add milk all at once; cook and stir till bubbly. Cook and stir 1 to 2 minutes more. Remove from heat. Add cheeses, stirring till almost melted.

Beat egg yolks till thick and lemon colored. Slowly add cheese mixture, stirring constantly. Cool slightly. Using *clean* beaters, beat egg whites till stiff peaks form. Gradually pour yolk mixture over beaten whites, folding to blend. Turn into an ungreased 1½-quart soufflé dish. Bake in a 300° oven for 1 hour or till a knife inserted near center comes out clean. Serve immediately. Serves 4.

Tip: Serve a soufflé immediately after it is removed from the oven; otherwise, it may fall. It's best to have your family or guests wait for the soufflé, because the soufflé won't wait for them.

To serve a soufflé, insert two forks back to back and pull the soufflé apart into individual servings. Then use a spoon to transfer the soufflé servings to warm plates.

ASPARAGUS OMELET

Provides 25% U.S. RDA of protein per serving—

- 1 10¾-ounce can condensed cream of asparagus soup
- ½ cup dairy sour cream
- 2 tablespoons milk
- ¼ teaspoon dried dillweed
- ½ pound asparagus, cut into 2-inch pieces
- 4 eggs, separated
- ¾ cup cream-style cottage cheese, drained
- 1 tablespoon butter *or* margarine

To make sauce, in a saucepan combine soup, sour cream, milk, and dillweed. Cook and stir over low heat till heated through. Keep warm. *Do not boil.*

In a covered saucepan cook asparagus in a small amount of boiling salted water 8 to 10 minutes or till tender. Drain well; keep warm. Beat egg whites till stiff peaks form (tips stand straight). Beat egg yolks at high speed of electric mixer about 5 minutes or till thick and lemon colored. Add cottage cheese, ¼ teaspoon *salt,* and ⅛ teaspoon *pepper;* beat till nearly smooth. Fold yolk mixture into beaten whites. To make omelet, in a 10-inch skillet with an oven-proof handle, heat butter till a drop of water sizzles in the skillet. Pour in egg mixture, mounding it slightly higher at the sides. Cook over low heat, uncovered, 8 to 10 minutes or till eggs are puffed and set, and the bottom is golden brown.

Place skillet in a 325° oven; bake 10 minutes or till a knife inserted near center comes out clean. Loosen sides of omelet. Make a shallow cut across the omelet, cutting slightly off-center. Spoon asparagus across the larger portion of omelet. Fold smaller portion over asparagus. Slip omelet onto a warm platter. Spoon some of the asparagus-sour-cream sauce atop the omelet; pass the remaining sauce. Makes 4 servings.

MONTEREY OMELET

Provides 29% U.S. RDA of protein per serving—

- 4 egg whites
- 2 tablespoons water
- ¼ teaspoon salt
- 4 egg yolks
- 1 tablespoon butter *or* margarine
- ½ cup fresh alfalfa sprouts
- ¾ cup shredded Monterey Jack cheese (3 ounces)
- ¼ cup broken walnuts, toasted
- ¼ cup cherry tomatoes, halved
- 2 tablespoons sliced pitted ripe olives
- Dairy sour cream *or* frozen avocado dip, thawed

Beat egg whites till frothy. Add water and salt; continue beating about 1½ minutes or till stiff peaks form. Beat egg yolks at high speed of electric mixer about 5 minutes or till thick and lemon colored. Fold egg yolks into egg whites.

To make omelet, in a 10-inch skillet with an oven-proof handle, heat the butter or margarine till a drop of water sizzles in the skillet. Pour in egg mixture, mounding it slightly higher at the sides. Cook over low heat, uncovered, for 8 to 10 minutes or till eggs are puffed and set, and the bottom is golden brown.

Place the skillet in a 325° oven; bake for 10 minutes or till a knife inserted near center comes out clean. Loosen sides of omelet with a metal spatula. Make a shallow cut across the omelet, cutting slightly off-center.

Sprinkle alfalfa sprouts across the larger portion of the omelet. Next sprinkle the Monterey Jack cheese, toasted walnuts, halved cherry tomatoes, and sliced ripe olives. Sprinkle with salt and pepper.

Fold the smaller portion of the omelet over the filling. Slip omelet onto a warm serving platter. Top with sour cream or avocado dip. Makes 3 servings.

SPICY PAELLA-STYLE VEGETABLES

Pictured on the cover
Provides 32% U.S. RDA of protein per serving—

- ¾ pound broccoli, sliced, *or* one 10-ounce package frozen chopped broccoli
- 2 small zucchini, sliced ¼ inch thick (2 cups)
- 2 medium green *or* red sweet peppers, chopped (1½ cups)
- ½ cup chopped onion
- 2 cloves garlic, minced
- ¼ cup olive oil *or* cooking oil
- 1 16-ounce can tomatoes, cut up
- 1 teaspoon salt
- ½ teaspoon ground red pepper
- ⅛ teaspoon pepper
- 2¾ cups chicken broth
- 1½ cups long grain rice
- 1 tablespoon lemon juice
- 1 cup shelled fresh *or* frozen peas, thawed
- ⅔ cup grated Parmesan cheese
- 6 eggs

Cook fresh broccoli in a small amount of boiling salted water for 5 minutes or till crisp-tender. (Or, if using frozen broccoli, cook according to package directions.) Drain. In a paella pan or a 12-inch oven-going skillet, cook zucchini, sweet pepper, onion, and garlic in olive oil till onion is tender. Stir in *undrained* tomatoes, salt, red pepper, and pepper. Stir in chicken broth, uncooked rice, and lemon juice; mix well. Bring to boiling.

Bake, covered, in a 350° oven for 10 minutes. Stir in broccoli, peas, and Parmesan cheese. Make 6 depressions in rice mixture with the back of a spoon. Carefully break the eggs into the depressions. Sprinkle eggs lightly with salt. Bake, covered, 15 to 18 minutes more or till eggs are set and rice is tender. Makes 6 servings.

Spicy Paella-Style Vegetables

OMELET CURRY

Provides 29% U.S. RDA of protein per serving—

- **2 tablespoons butter *or* margarine**
- **1 teaspoon curry powder**
- **2 tablespoons all-purpose flour**
- **¼ teaspoon salt**
- **Dash pepper**
- **1 cup milk**
- **4 egg whites**
- **2 tablespoons water**
- **¼ teaspoon salt**
- **4 egg yolks**
- **1 tablespoon butter *or* margarine**
- **1 small tomato, chopped**
- **½ cup chopped peanuts**
- **¼ cup raisins**
- **2 tablespoons snipped parsley**
- **2 tablespoons coconut, toasted (optional)**

To make sauce, in a saucepan melt 2 tablespoons butter or margarine. Stir in curry; cook 1 minute. Stir in flour, ¼ teaspoon salt, and pepper. Add milk all at once. Cook and stir till thickened and bubbly. Cook and stir 1 to 2 minutes more.

Beat egg whites till frothy. Add water and ¼ teaspoon salt; continue beating about 1½ minutes or till stiff peaks form. Beat egg yolks at high speed of electric mixer about 5 minutes or till thick and lemon colored. Fold egg yolks into egg whites.

In a 10-inch skillet with an oven-proof handle, heat 1 tablespoon butter or margarine till a drop of water sizzles on the skillet. Pour in egg mixture, mounding it slightly higher at the sides. Cook over low heat, uncovered, for 8 to 10 minutes or till eggs are puffed and set, and bottom is golden brown.

Place skillet in a 325° oven; bake for 10 minutes or till a knife inserted near center comes out clean. Loosen sides of the omelet. Make a shallow cut across the omelet, cutting slightly off-center.

To *half* of the sauce add tomato, peanuts, raisins, and parsley. Set aside remaining half; keep warm. Spread the tomato sauce mixture over the larger portion of the omelet. Fold the smaller portion over the filling. Slip omelet onto a warm serving platter. Pour reserved sauce over the omelet. If desired, sprinkle with toasted coconut. Makes 3 servings.

CLASSIC CHEESE STRATA

Provides 30% U.S. RDA of protein per serving—

- **8 slices day-old bread**
- **8 ounces American *or* Swiss cheese, sliced**
- **4 eggs**
- **2½ cups milk**
- **¼ cup finely chopped onion**
- **1½ teaspoons salt**
- **½ teaspoon prepared mustard**
- **Dash pepper**
- **Paprika**

Trim the crusts from *4 slices* of the bread. Cut the trimmed slices in half diagonally to make 8 triangles; set aside.

Arrange the trimmings and the remaining 4 slices of untrimmed bread to cover the bottom of a 9x9x2-inch baking pan. Place American or Swiss cheese slices over the bread in the baking pan. Arrange the reserved 8 bread triangles in 2 rows over the cheese. (Points will slightly overlap bases of adjacent triangles.)

Thoroughly beat the eggs; stir in the milk, finely chopped onion, salt, prepared mustard, and pepper. Pour the egg mixture over bread and cheese layers in the baking pan. Sprinkle with paprika. Cover; let chill in refrigerator several hours or overnight. Bake, uncovered, in a 325° oven for 1¼ hours or till a knife inserted near center comes out clean. Let stand 10 minutes before serving. Serves 6.

SWISS-SAUERKRAUT STRATA

Provides 32% U.S. RDA of protein per serving—

  6 slices rye bread, toasted
  4 beaten eggs
  2 cups milk
  1 teaspoon salt
  ½ teaspoon caraway seed
  2 cups shredded Swiss cheese
  2 tablespoons chopped pimiento
  **1 8-ounce can sauerkraut, rinsed,
     drained, and snipped**
  Snipped parsley (optional)

Cut toasted bread into ½-inch cubes; set aside. In a large bowl combine beaten eggs, milk, salt, and caraway seed. Stir in bread cubes, *1½ cups* of the Swiss cheese, and the chopped pimiento. Spread sauerkraut in an 8x8x2-inch baking dish. Spoon egg-bread mixture over sauerkraut.

Cover and refrigerate at least 1 hour. Bake in a 350° oven for 45 to 50 minutes. Sprinkle with remaining Swiss cheese. Bake 5 minutes longer or till a knife inserted near center comes out clean. Let stand 10 minutes before serving. Sprinkle with parsley, if desired. Makes 6 servings.

CHEESY EGG BAKE

Provides 27% U.S. RDA of protein per serving—

  **1 10¾-ounce can condensed cream
     of chicken soup**
  ¼ cup milk
  2 tablespoons finely chopped onion
  ½ teaspoon prepared mustard
  1½ cups shredded Swiss cheese
  6 eggs
  **6 ½-inch-thick slices French bread,
     buttered and halved**
  Snipped parsley

In a saucepan combine soup, milk, onion, and mustard; cook and stir till heated through. Remove from heat; stir in cheese till melted. Pour *1 cup* of the soup mixture into a 10x6x2-inch baking dish. Carefully break eggs atop soup mixture in baking dish. Spoon remaining soup mixture around eggs. Stand bread halves around baking dish edges, crust side up. Bake, uncovered, in a 350° oven about 20 minutes or till eggs are set to desired doneness. Sprinkle with parsley. To serve, spoon soup mixture over eggs and bread slices. Makes 6 servings.

MEXICAN-STYLE CHEESE STRATA

Provides 32% U.S. RDA of protein per serving—

  **4 cups cheese-flavored tortilla
     chips, broken**
  **2 cups shredded Monterey Jack
     cheese (8 ounces)**
  6 eggs
  2½ cups milk
  **1 4-ounce can green chili peppers,
     rinsed, seeded, and chopped**
  ¼ cup finely chopped onion
  3 tablespoons catsup
  ½ teaspoon salt
  ¼ teaspoon bottled hot pepper sauce
  **Whole cheese-flavored tortilla
     chips**
  Tomato slices, halved

Sprinkle broken tortilla chips evenly over the bottom of a greased 12x7x2-inch baking dish. Sprinkle with cheese. In a medium bowl use a rotary beater to beat together eggs, milk, chili peppers, onion, catsup, salt, and hot pepper sauce; pour over cheese in dish. Cover; refrigerate several hours or overnight.

Bake, uncovered, in a 325° oven for 50 to 55 minutes or till a knife inserted near center comes out clean. Garnish with whole tortilla chips and halved tomato slices. Makes 6 servings.

HERBS · & · SPICES

Basil

Bay Leaves

Caraway

Chives

Individual tastes differ so much when it comes to herbs and spices that it would be presumptuous to specify hard and fast rules for using them. That's why the uses we list with each spice or herb description are only suggestions. You may find that you enjoy using spices and herbs in other ways, too.

If a spice or herb is one that you have not tried before, start by adding only a very small amount. Remember, it's easier to add more if you've used too little than to take some out if you've used too much. Spices and herbs should enhance the flavor of food—not overpower it.

Fresh herbs can easily be substituted for dried. As a general rule of thumb when substituting snipped or chopped fresh herbs for dried herbs, triple the amount specified in the recipe.

Basil is also called sweet basil. It has an aromatic clovelike aroma and is frequently blended with other herbs in seasoning foods such as stews, stuffings, vegetables, pasta, salads, salad dressings, stewed fruits, breads, and sauces.

Bay leaves are also called laurel leaves. The distinct, strong, pungent, almost-bitter flavor increases with the amount used and the cooking time. Bay leaves complement the flavor of stews, dry bean dishes, potatoes, rice, salads, egg dishes, and marinades.

Caraway seed are small brown crescent-

Dill

Fennel

Garlic

Marjoram

shaped seed with a distinctive pleasant flavor that has a sweet undertone. They should be used sparingly in stews, stuffings, vegetables, salads, breads, egg dishes, dips, and spreads.

Chives are the leaves of a hollow grasslike plant that lend an oniony flavor to foods. Chives go well with stews, casseroles, vegetables, salads, dressings, and gravies.

Dill is available as either seed or weed (leaves of a dill plant). Dill seeds are flat, oval, and light brown. Dillweed is bright green and fernlike. The seeds have a pungent and aromatic flavor, while the weed has a delicate, more subtle flavor. Dill complements stews, vegetables, dressings, egg dishes, and sauces.

Fennel seed are oval, yellowish-brown seed that have the slight flavor of licorice. Fennel is a good addition to stews, vegetables, salads, dressings, breads, sauces, and egg dishes.

Garlic is available in many forms—fresh, powder, salt, minced dried, and juice. All of them lend a strong and pungent flavor to foods such as casseroles, stews, vegetables, salads, dressings, sauces, and marinades.

Marjoram is available either ground or dried. Its gray-green leaves have an aromatic and pleasant flavor with bitter undertones. Marjoram should be used sparingly at first and increased to taste in foods such as casseroles, vegetables, salads, egg dishes, and sauces.

70

Mint

Oregano

Parsley

Rosemary

Mint is the dried leaf of the spearmint plant and is available as flakes or in extract form. Sometimes you also can find fresh mint sprigs. It has a sweet flavor with a cool aftertaste. Use mint with vegetables, salads, stewed fruits, marinades, hot beverages, and sauces.

Oregano is available as both dried and ground leaves. Both have a strong and aromatic taste with a strong, bitter aftertaste. Use oregano with stews, casseroles, soups, vegetables, salads, main dishes, and egg dishes.

Parsley is used both fresh and dried as a garnish for foods. Since it has a very mild flavor, it blends well with other herbs. Use it in almost any food with the exception of sweets.

Rosemary has a distinctive, fresh, sweet, pinewood flavor. Its gray-green leaves resemble miniature curved pine needles. Include rosemary in dishes such as stews, soups, casseroles, vegetables, breads, main dishes, and egg dishes.

Sage is very aromatic and slightly bitter. It is available ground or as leaves, and should be used sparingly in stews, soups, stuffings, main dishes, egg dishes, breads, and sauces.

Savory has an aromatic piquant flavor. Add these brownish green leaves sparingly to stews, soups, casseroles, stuffings, vegetables, sauces, main dishes, and egg dishes.

Tarragon leaves are slender and dark green,

Sage

Savory

Tarragon

Thyme

with a slightly astringent flavor. Use tarragon in casseroles, stews, soups, salads, dressings, egg dishes, cheese spreads, main dishes, and sauces.

Thyme leaves are grayish-green and have a warm, aromatic, slightly pungent flavor. Add to soups, casseroles, vegetables, salads, breads, entrées, egg dishes, sauces, and spreads.

These herbs and spices are just a few of the dozens that are available to enhance the foods you cook. Experiment with them and see how they can add new flavors to your cooking. Then try the many other herbs and spices that are available to you.

In addition to their seasoning uses, spices and herbs can make attractive garnishes, too.

Use a sprig of fresh mint to perk up a fruit salad, a frozen dessert, or a cool beverage.

Fresh dill is an attractive addition to a main dish or vegetable platter.

Snipped chives add interest and flavor to cottage cheese, vegetables, stews, and soups.

Snipped parsley or parsley sprigs are a quick and easy garnish for main dishes, casseroles, and vegetables.

Snipped fresh basil is attractive and delicious on tomato slices.

Use cinnamon sticks, whole cloves, and ground nutmeg to add flavor and eye appeal to hot beverages and fruit compotes.

And paprika adds color to egg dishes, vegetables, and sauces.

71

TOFU-BROCCOLI STRATA

Provides 27% U.S. RDA of protein per serving—

 1 10-ounce package frozen
     chopped broccoli
 2 cups cubed day-old bread
 4 ounces sliced Swiss cheese
 8 ounces fresh tofu (bean curd),
     drained and cut into ½-inch
     cubes
 2 tablespoons chopped pimiento,
     drained
 4 ounces sliced Swiss cheese
 2 cups cubed day-old bread
 4 eggs
1¾ cups milk
1¼ teaspoons salt
     Dash ground red pepper
 1 cup cubed day-old bread
 2 tablespoons butter *or* margarine,
     melted

In a medium saucepan cook chopped broccoli, covered, in a small amount of boiling salted water for 3 minutes; drain well. Place the 2 cups bread cubes on the bottom of an ungreased 8x8x2-inch baking dish. Top the bread cubes with 4 ounces sliced Swiss cheese. Top the Swiss cheese with all the cooked broccoli, cubed tofu, and chopped pimiento. Place 4 ounces sliced Swiss cheese and the 2 cups bread cubes atop.

In a bowl thoroughly beat the eggs; stir in the milk, salt, and ground red pepper. Pour the egg mixture over the ingredients in the baking dish. Cover and chill for 1 to 3 hours.

Toss the 1 cup bread cubes with the melted butter or margarine. Sprinkle atop the chilled mixture. Bake, uncovered, in a 325° oven for 55 to 60 minutes or till a knife inserted near center comes out clean. Let stand 10 minutes before serving. Makes 8 servings.

ZUCCHINI-MUSHROOM STRATA

Provides 33% U.S. RDA of protein per serving—

 2 cups sliced fresh mushrooms
 1 medium zucchini, sliced
     (1¼ cups)
 6 slices bread, toasted and cut
     into quarters
 1 cup shredded American cheese
     (4 ounces)
 1 cup shredded Swiss cheese
     (4 ounces)
¼ cup chopped pimiento, drained
 2 tablespoons finely chopped
     onion
 4 eggs
 2 cups milk
 2 tablespoons all-purpose flour
½ teaspoon salt
½ teaspoon dried basil, crushed
¼ cup slivered almonds, toasted

In a medium saucepan cook sliced mushrooms and zucchini, covered, in a small amount of boiling salted water for 5 minutes; drain well. Arrange *half* of the toasted bread quarters in the bottom of a 9x9x2-inch baking pan. Top with the shredded American cheese, then the cooked zucchini and mushroom mixture. Sprinkle the shredded Swiss cheese, chopped pimiento, and the finely chopped onion over the zucchini and mushroom layer. Top with remaining toasted bread quarters.

In a bowl thoroughly beat the eggs; stir in the milk, flour, salt, and basil. Pour the egg mixture over toasted bread and vegetables in the baking pan. Cover and chill at least 1 hour.

Sprinkle toasted almonds over chilled mixture. Bake, uncovered, in a 325° oven about 50 minutes or till a knife inserted near center comes out clean. Let stand 10 minutes before serving. Serves 6.

72

BROCCOLI SCRAMBLE CASSEROLE

Provides 31% U.S. RDA of protein per serving —

¾ pound broccoli *or* one 10-ounce
    package frozen broccoli spears
6 eggs
⅓ cup milk
    Dash pepper
2 tablespoons butter *or*
    margarine
1 10¾-ounce can condensed
    cream of chicken soup
½ cup cream-style cottage cheese
1 tablespoon all-purpose flour
¼ teaspoon dried tarragon,
    crushed
¾ cup soft bread crumbs (1 slice)
1 tablespoon butter *or* margarine,
    melted

If using fresh broccoli, wash broccoli and cut into spears. Split stalks almost to flowerets. Cook, covered, in boiling salted water 10 to 15 minutes or just till tender. (*Or,* if using frozen broccoli, cook according to package directions.) Drain. In a 10x6x2-inch baking dish, arrange broccoli with stems toward center; set aside. In a blender container combine eggs, milk, and dash pepper. Cover and blend well. In a 10-inch skillet heat 2 tablespoons butter. Pour the egg mixture over hot butter. Reduce heat; cook till eggs are set but still glossy and moist, lifting and turning cooked portions with a metal spatula. Spoon eggs atop broccoli. In a blender container combine soup, cottage cheese, flour, and tarragon. Cover and blend till smooth; pour into a small saucepan. Cook and stir till bubbly. Cook and stir 1 to 2 minutes more. Pour over eggs and broccoli. Toss bread crumbs with 1 tablespoon melted butter; sprinkle atop. Bake, uncovered, in a 350° oven for 20 minutes. Makes 4 servings.

BAKED CHILIES RELLENOS

Provides 29% U.S. RDA of protein per serving —

2 4-ounce cans green chili peppers
    (6 chili peppers)
6 ounces Monterey Jack cheese
4 beaten eggs
⅓ cup milk
½ cup all-purpose flour
½ teaspoon baking powder
½ teaspoon salt
1 cup shredded cheddar cheese
    (4 ounces)
1 16-ounce can tomatoes, drained
    and cut up
¼ cup chopped onion
1 tablespoon snipped parsley
1 teaspoon instant beef bouillon
    granules
¼ teaspoon chili powder
⅛ teaspoon ground cinnamon
⅛ teaspoon pepper
½ cup dairy sour cream

Drain and rinse peppers; halve lengthwise and remove seeds. Cut the Monterey Jack cheese into strips to fit inside peppers. Line the inside of *each* pepper half with a strip of Monterey Jack cheese; place in a greased 10x6x2-inch baking dish.

In a mixing bowl combine eggs and milk; stir in flour, baking powder, and salt. Pour egg mixture over peppers. Sprinkle shredded cheddar cheese atop. Bake in a 350° oven about 30 minutes or till golden.

Meanwhile, to make sauce, in a saucepan combine tomatoes, onion, parsley, beef bouillon granules, chili powder, cinnamon, and pepper. Bring to boiling; reduce heat. Simmer, uncovered, for 5 minutes. Cover and keep warm over low heat till baked chili peppers are done.

Serve baked chili peppers with warm sauce spooned atop. Top each serving with a dollop of sour cream. Serves 6.

Red Beans and
Cheese Corn Bread

RED BEANS AND CHEESE CORN BREAD

Provides 35% U.S. RDA of protein per serving—

- 2 cups yellow cornmeal
- ½ cup all-purpose flour
- 1 tablespoon baking powder
- 1 tablespoon sugar
- 1 teaspoon baking soda
- 2 beaten eggs
- 2½ cups milk
- 2 tablespoons cooking oil
- 1 cup shredded cheddar *or* Monterey Jack cheese with jalapeño peppers (4 ounces)
- 1 8¾-ounce can whole kernel corn, drained
- ½ cup chopped red *or* green pepper
- 1 medium onion, chopped (½ cup)
- 1 tablespoon butter *or* margarine
- 1 15½-ounce can red kidney beans
- 1 8-ounce can tomato sauce
- 1 teaspoon chili powder
- 1 teaspoon Worcestershire sauce
  Dash bottled hot pepper sauce
- 2 cups shredded cheddar *or* Monterey Jack cheese with jalapeño peppers (8 ounces)

Stir together cornmeal, flour, baking powder, sugar, baking soda, and 1¼ teaspoons *salt*. Combine eggs, milk, and oil. Add all at once to dry ingredients. Beat just till smooth. Fold in the 1 cup cheese, corn, and red or green pepper. Turn into a greased 9x9x2-inch baking pan. Bake in a 400° oven 35 to 40 minutes or till golden. Meanwhile, cook onion in butter till tender. Stir in *undrained* beans, tomato sauce, chili powder, Worcestershire sauce, hot pepper sauce, and ¼ teaspoon *salt*. Simmer, uncovered, about 8 minutes or till heated through. Mash beans slightly. Cut corn bread into 8 squares. Spoon bean mixture atop each square. Top *each* with ¼ *cup* cheese. Makes 8 servings.

SOYBEAN CASSEROLE

Provides 28% U.S. RDA of protein per serving—

- ½ cup dry soybeans
- ½ cup dry lima beans
- 1 cup chopped celery
- 1 medium onion, chopped
- 1 large green pepper, chopped
- 2 cloves garlic, minced
- 3 tablespoons cooking oil
- 1 16-ounce can tomatoes, cut up
- 1 6-ounce can tomato paste
- ¼ cup dry red wine
- 1 bay leaf
- 1 teaspoon dried marjoram, crushed
- 1 teaspoon instant beef bouillon granules
- ⅛ teaspoon bottled hot pepper sauce
- 1 cup packaged biscuit mix
- ¾ cup shredded cheddar cheese
- 1 tablespoon toasted wheat germ
- ⅓ cup milk

Rinse beans; place in a heavy saucepan with 3 cups *water*. Add 1 teaspoon *salt*. Cover; soak overnight. Freeze *undrained* beans in saucepan or freezer container. Thaw. Simmer, covered, 45 minutes or till beans are tender. Add water as necessary. Drain, reserving ⅔ cup liquid.

Cook celery, onion, green pepper, and garlic in cooking oil till tender. Stir in *undrained* tomatoes, tomato paste, wine, bay leaf, marjoram, beef bouillon granules, hot pepper sauce, and ⅛ teaspoon *pepper*. Bring to boiling; reduce heat. Cover; simmer 15 minutes. Stir in beans and reserved liquid; heat through. Remove bay leaf.

In a mixing bowl toss together biscuit mix, cheese, and wheat germ. Add milk all at once; stir just till moistened.

Turn soybean mixture into a 2-quart casserole. Drop biscuit mixture atop, making 10 mounds. Bake in a 350° oven 30 minutes or till golden. Serves 5.

CALIFORNIA QUICHE CASSEROLE

Provides 28% U.S. RDA of protein per serving —

2 cups coarsely shredded zucchini (about 2 medium)
½ cup chopped onion
4 beaten eggs
1½ cups milk
1 tablespoon all-purpose flour
¼ teaspoon salt
⅛ teaspoon ground nutmeg
⅛ teaspoon pepper
1½ cups shredded Monterey Jack cheese (6 ounces)
1 4-ounce can sliced mushrooms, drained
1 8-ounce can stewed tomatoes, finely cut up
1 teaspoon cornstarch
¼ teaspoon dried oregano, crushed
Dash salt

To make quiche, in a covered saucepan cook shredded zucchini and chopped onion in a small amount of boiling salted water for 5 minutes; drain well, pressing out excess liquid. In a bowl combine beaten eggs, milk, flour, the ¼ teaspoon salt, nutmeg, and pepper; mix well. Stir in shredded Monterey Jack cheese, mushrooms, and zucchini-onion mixture. Pour into an ungreased 10x6x2-inch baking dish. Place the baking dish in a large baking pan; pour hot water into the large baking pan to a depth of 1 inch. Bake in a 325° oven about 60 minutes or till a knife inserted near center comes out clean. Let stand 10 minutes before serving.

Meanwhile, to make tomato sauce, in a small saucepan combine *undrained* tomatoes, cornstarch, oregano, and dash salt. Cook and stir till tomato mixture is thickened and bubbly. Cook and stir 1 to 2 minutes more. To serve, spoon tomato sauce over quiche. Makes 5 servings.

CHEESY EGGPLANT PARMIGIANA

Provides 32% U.S. RDA of protein per serving —

¾ cup sliced fresh mushrooms
¼ cup chopped green onion
2 tablespoons butter *or* margarine
1 16-ounce can tomatoes, cut up
½ cup dry white wine
½ teaspoon dried oregano, crushed
½ teaspoon dried basil, crushed
½ teaspoon sugar
¼ teaspoon salt
2 tablespoons cornstarch
2 tablespoons snipped parsley
¼ cup all-purpose flour
½ teaspoon salt
1 medium eggplant, cut crosswise into ½-inch slices
1 beaten egg
½ cup olive oil *or* cooking oil
½ cup grated Parmesan cheese
6 ounces sliced mozzarella cheese, cut into triangles

For sauce, in a saucepan cook mushrooms and onion in butter till tender but not brown. Stir in *undrained* tomatoes, wine, oregano, basil, sugar, and the ¼ teaspoon salt. Bring to boiling; reduce heat. Simmer, uncovered, 10 minutes. Combine 2 tablespoons cold *water* and cornstarch; stir into tomato mixture. Cook and stir till thickened and bubbly. Cook and stir 1 to 2 minutes more. Stir in parsley.

Combine flour and the ½ teaspoon salt. Dip eggplant slices in beaten egg, then in flour mixture. In a large skillet brown the eggplant in hot oil, half of the slices at a time. Drain on paper toweling. Arrange eggplant in a 13x9x2-inch baking dish, overlapping slices to fit. Sprinkle with Parmesan cheese. Top with tomato sauce and mozzarella cheese. Bake in a 400° oven about 20 minutes or till heated through and cheese is melted. Serves 4.

CHEESY WALNUT-STUFFED PEPPERS

Provides 35% U.S. RDA of protein per serving—

- 3 large green peppers
- ½ cup chopped onion
- 1 clove garlic, minced
- 1 tablespoon butter *or* margarine
- 4 beaten eggs
- 2 cups cooked long grain rice
- 2 cups shredded cheddar cheese (8 ounces)
- 1 cup chopped walnuts
- ¼ teaspoon salt
- 2 tablespoons butter *or* margarine
- 2 tablespoons all-purpose flour
- ½ teaspoon dried sage, crushed
- ¼ teaspoon salt
- ⅛ teaspoon pepper
- 1¼ cups milk
- 2 tablespoons snipped parsley
- 1 tablespoon chopped pimiento, drained

Cut tops from green peppers. Cut peppers in half lengthwise; discard seeds and membrane. Cook in boiling salted water for 3 to 5 minutes; invert to drain.

Cook onion and garlic in the 1 tablespoon butter till tender but not brown. In a mixing bowl combine eggs, cooked rice, shredded cheese, chopped nuts, salt, and onion mixture; mix well.

Season green pepper shells with salt and pepper. Fill peppers with the rice mixture. Place in a 13x9x2-inch baking dish. Bake, covered, in a 350° oven for 25 to 30 minutes or till heated through.

Meanwhile, to make sauce, in a saucepan melt 2 tablespoons butter or margarine. Stir in flour, sage, salt, and pepper. Add milk all at once. Cook and stir till thickened and bubbly. Cook and stir 1 to 2 minutes more. Stir in snipped parsley and chopped pimiento. Serve sauce over stuffed peppers. Makes 6 servings.

VEGETABLE NUT LOAF

Provides 33% U.S. RDA of protein per serving—

- 1 cup finely chopped carrot
- ½ cup finely chopped onion
- ½ cup finely chopped green pepper
- 1 clove garlic, minced
- 3 tablespoons butter *or* margarine
- ¼ cup all-purpose flour
- ¾ teaspoon salt
- ¾ teaspoon dried thyme, crushed
- ⅛ teaspoon pepper
- 1 cup milk
- 1½ cups shredded Monterey Jack cheese *or* cheddar cheese (6 ounces)
- 1¼ cups chopped walnuts *or* chopped almonds
- ¾ cup toasted wheat germ
- 3 slightly beaten eggs
  Toasted wheat germ
  Dairy sour cream
  Snipped parsley (optional)

In a large saucepan cook carrot, onion, green pepper, and garlic in butter or margarine till onion is tender but not brown. Stir in the flour, salt, thyme, and pepper. Add the milk all at once. Cook and stir till thickened and bubbly. Cook and stir 1 to 2 minutes more. Remove from heat. Stir in the shredded cheese, walnuts or almonds, and the ¾ cup wheat germ, stirring till cheese is melted. Slowly stir the hot cheese mixture into the beaten eggs, stirring constantly.

Sprinkle the bottom and sides of a well-greased 8x4x2-inch or 9x5x3-inch loaf pan with additional wheat germ. Turn vegetable mixture into prepared pan. Bake in a 350° oven for 40 minutes or till well browned and firm. Let stand 10 minutes before serving. Remove from pan. To serve, cut into thick slices. Top *each* slice with a dollop of sour cream. If desired, garnish *each* serving with snipped parsley. Makes 6 servings.

CARAWAY EGG AND CHEESE CREPES

Provides 31% U.S. RDA of protein per serving—

     1 cup milk
     ¾ cup all-purpose flour
     1 egg
     ¼ cup toasted wheat germ
     1 tablespoon cooking oil
     ¼ teaspoon salt
     6 beaten eggs
     ¾ cup cream-style cottage cheese
     1 tablespoon snipped parsley
     ½ teaspoon salt
     4 tablespoons butter *or* margarine
     ¼ cup sliced green onion
     2 tablespoons all-purpose flour
     ⅛ teaspoon salt
       Dash pepper
  1¼ cups milk
     ½ cup shredded Monterey Jack
       cheese with caraway (2 ounces)

To make crepes, combine milk, the ¾ cup flour, the 1 egg, wheat germ, oil, and the ¼ teaspoon salt; beat till smooth. Heat a lightly greased 6-inch skillet. Remove from heat; spoon in about 2 tablespoons batter. Lift and tilt skillet to spread batter. Return to heat; brown crepe on one side only. (Or, cook crepes on an inverted crepe pan according to manufacturer's directions.) Invert pan over paper toweling; loosen crepe with a spatula. Repeat cooking with the remaining batter to make 12 crepes, greasing skillet occasionally. Set crepes aside.

In a mixing bowl combine the 6 beaten eggs, cottage cheese, parsley, and the ½ teaspoon salt. In a 10-inch skillet melt 2 *tablespoons* of the butter or margarine. Pour egg mixture over hot butter or margarine; reduce heat. Cook without stirring till egg mixture begins to set on bottom and around edges. Lift and fold the partially cooked egg mixture so the uncooked portion flows underneath. Continue cooking for 5 minutes or till egg mixture is set but still moist and glossy.

Place about ¼ cup of the egg mixture in the center of the unbrowned side of *each* crepe. Fold crepe ends over. Place, seam side down, in a 12x7½x2-inch baking dish. Cover; bake in a 375° oven for 18 to 20 minutes or till heated through.

For sauce, cook green onion in remaining 2 tablespoons butter or margarine till tender. Stir in the 2 tablespoons flour, ⅛ teaspoon salt, and dash pepper. Add the 1¼ cups milk all at once. Cook and stir till thickened and bubbly. Cook and stir 1 to 2 minutes more. Remove from heat. Add shredded cheese, stirring till melted. Pour sauce over crepes. Serves 6.

HERBED LENTILS AND RICE

Provides 32% U.S. RDA of protein per serving—

  2⅔ cups chicken broth
     ¾ cup dry lentils
     ¾ cup chopped onion
     ½ cup brown rice
     ¼ cup dry white wine
     ½ teaspoon dried basil, crushed
     ¼ teaspoon salt
     ¼ teaspoon dried oregano, crushed
     ¼ teaspoon dried thyme, crushed
     ⅛ teaspoon garlic powder
     ⅛ teaspoon pepper
     4 ounces Swiss cheese

Combine chicken broth, lentils, onion, uncooked rice, wine, and seasonings. Shred *half* of the cheese; stir into lentil mixture. Turn into an ungreased 1½-quart casserole. Bake, covered, in a 350° oven for 1½ to 2 hours or till lentils and rice are done, stirring twice. Cut remaining cheese into 8 strips. Uncover casserole; top with cheese strips. Bake 2 to 3 minutes more or till cheese is melted. Makes 4 servings.

Herbed Lentils and Rice

GREEN AND WHITE LASAGNA

Provides 31% U.S. RDA of protein per serving—

- **6 ounces lasagna noodles**
- **1 cup finely chopped onion**
- **1 cup finely chopped celery**
- **2 cloves garlic, minced**
- **1 tablespoon cooking oil**
- **2 tablespoons all-purpose flour**
- **2 teaspoons dried basil, crushed**
- **2 teaspoons dried oregano, crushed**
- **¾ teaspoon salt**
- **½ teaspoon pepper**
- **2 10-ounce packages frozen cut broccoli, thawed**
- **1 cup light cream *or* milk**
- **3 cups shredded Gouda cheese**
- **1 3-ounce package cream cheese, cut into ½-inch cubes**
- **½ cup dry white wine**
- **1½ cups cream-style cottage cheese**
- **1 slightly beaten egg**
- **8 ounces sliced mozzarella cheese**
- **¼ cup grated Parmesan cheese**

In a large saucepan cook lasagna noodles according to package directions; drain. Set aside. In a large skillet cook onion, celery, and garlic in oil till vegetables are tender but not brown. Stir in flour, basil, oregano, salt, and pepper. Add broccoli and cream. Cook and stir till thickened and bubbly. Cook and stir 1 to 2 minutes longer. Add Gouda and cream cheese, stirring over low heat till melted. Stir in wine. Remove from heat.

Combine cottage cheese and egg. Layer *half* of the noodles in a greased 13x9x2-inch baking dish. Top with *half* of the broccoli mixture, *half* of the cottage cheese mixture, *half* of the mozzarella cheese, and *half* of the Parmesan. Repeat layers. Bake, uncovered, in a 375° oven for 30 to 35 minutes. Let stand 10 minutes before serving. Makes 12 servings.

VEGETABLE-WHEAT-GERM SCALLOP

Provides 32% U.S. RDA of protein per serving—

- **4 cups coarsely shredded cabbage**
- **2 cups sliced carrots**
- **1 cup water**
- **1 medium onion, thinly sliced**
- **1 small green pepper, diced**
- **3 tablespoons butter *or* margarine**
- **3 tablespoons all-purpose flour**
- **2 teaspoons instant chicken bouillon granules**
- **1 cup shredded mozzarella cheese (4 ounces)**
- **1 cup shredded fontina cheese (4 ounces)**
- **¼ cup grated Parmesan cheese**
- **⅓ cup toasted wheat germ**
- **¼ cup fine dry bread crumbs**
- **¼ cup shelled pumpkin seed**
- **2 tablespoons butter *or* margarine, melted**

In a large saucepan cook cabbage and carrots in water about 10 minutes or till nearly tender. Drain well, reserving the liquid. Add enough water to the reserved liquid to measure 1 cup total liquid. Set liquid and vegetables aside.

Cook onion and green pepper in the 3 tablespoons butter or margarine till onion is tender but not brown. Stir in flour and bouillon granules; add the reserved 1 cup liquid. Cook and stir till thickened and bubbly. Cook and stir 1 to 2 minutes more. Remove from heat. Add the vegetables, the mozzarella, fontina, and Parmesan cheeses, stirring till cheeses are melted.

Turn vegetable mixture into a 1½-quart casserole. Combine the wheat germ, bread crumbs, pumpkin seed, and the 2 tablespoons melted butter; sprinkle atop vegetable mixture. Bake in a 375° oven for 20 to 25 minutes or till hot and bubbly. Let stand 10 minutes. Makes 5 servings.

GREEK CASSEROLE

Provides 35% U.S. RDA of protein per serving—

    1 cup elbow macaroni
   ⅓ cup grated Parmesan cheese
  2¼ cups milk
    1 beaten egg
   ½ cup chopped onion
   ¼ cup chopped green pepper
    1 clove garlic, minced
    2 tablespoons cooking oil
    1 7½-ounce can tomatoes, cut up
   ½ teaspoon ground cinnamon
   ⅛ teaspoon ground nutmeg
   ¼ cup butter *or* margarine
   ¼ cup all-purpose flour
    1 beaten egg
   ½ cup grated Parmesan cheese
    1 10-ounce package frozen
       chopped spinach, cooked and
       drained

Cook macaroni according to package directions; drain. Stir in the ⅓ cup Parmesan cheese, ¼ *cup* of the milk, and the 1 beaten egg; set aside.

Cook onion, green pepper, and garlic in oil till tender. Stir in *undrained* tomatoes, cinnamon, nutmeg, ½ teaspoon *salt,* and ⅛ teaspoon *pepper.* Cook, uncovered, stirring occasionally till most of the liquid is evaporated. Set aside.

Melt butter; stir in flour and ¼ teaspoon *salt.* Add remaining 2 cups milk. Cook and stir till bubbly. Cook and stir 1 to 2 minutes more. Stir *half* of the hot mixture into beaten egg; return all to saucepan. Stir in the ½ cup Parmesan. Stir ¾ *cup* of the Parmesan mixture into spinach.

Layer *half* of the macaroni mixture in the bottom of an 8x8x2-inch baking pan. Spoon onion mixture atop, then top with spinach mixture, spreading to cover. Top with remaining macaroni mixture. Spread remaining Parmesan mixture over all. Bake in a 350° oven about 45 minutes. Let stand 10 minutes. Makes 4 servings.

CHEESE, GRITS, AND BEAN BAKE

Provides 35% U.S. RDA of protein per serving—

    3 cups water
   ¾ cup quick-cooking white grits
    1 6-ounce link cheese spread with
       bacon, cut up
    2 tablespoons butter *or* margarine
    2 beaten eggs
   ½ cup milk
   ½ cup shredded cheddar cheese
       (2 ounces)
    1 15½-ounce can red kidney beans,
       drained
    1 15-ounce can garbanzo beans,
       drained
    1 cup chopped celery
   ¾ cup chopped green pepper
   ¾ cup tomato juice
   ¼ cup cooking oil
   ¼ cup vinegar
    1 1¼-ounce envelope chili
       seasoning mix
    1 cup cherry tomatoes, halved

Bring water and 1 teaspoon *salt* to boiling; stir in grits. Return to boiling. Reduce heat; cook, uncovered, about 5 minutes, stirring often. Remove from heat. Add cheese spread and butter, stirring till melted. Combine eggs and milk. Stir *half* of the grits mixture into egg mixture. Return all to saucepan. Turn mixture into a buttered 12x7½x2-inch baking dish. Bake in a 350° oven 30 to 35 minutes or till a knife inserted near center comes out clean. Sprinkle with cheddar cheese. Bake 1 to 2 minutes more. Let stand 10 minutes.

Meanwhile, combine kidney beans, garbanzo beans, celery, green pepper, tomato juice, oil, vinegar, and chili seasoning. Heat through, stirring occasionally. Stir in tomatoes; heat through. Spoon *some* of the bean mixture around edge of the casserole. Pass remainder. Serves 6.

UNUSUAL·VEGETABLES

Add variety to your meals with vegetables. Use the following key and diagram to identify some unusual vegetables.

1 Curly endive is a frilly-leaved green with a slightly bitter flavor.

2 Bok choy looks like celery, but its flavor is more like cabbage.

3 Artichokes should be heavy with tightly packed leaves and no brown spots.

4 Savoy cabbage has compact heads of wrinkled, curled leaves, while (**5**) **red cabbage** has red leaves. Look for tightly packed heads that are heavy.

6 New potatoes should be firm and have shallow eyes. Avoid any that are cut, sprouted, green, or blemished.

7 Pattypan squash should be heavy and have a rind that yields to gentle pressure.

8 Okra pods can be smooth or ridged. Avoid any pods that are dull or shriveled.

9 Beets with greens should have a smooth globular shape and a rich red color. Avoid large, soft, or shriveled beets. The appearance of the beet tops (greens) does not affect the beet. However, if you use the greens, choose those that are crisp, fresh, and free from defects.

10 Black-eyed peas should have crisp, full pods. Avoid yellow or swollen pods.

11 Jicama is a potatolike vegetable with a rough, brown skin and a white interior.

12 Yellow crookneck squash should be heavy and have a rind that yields to gentle pressure.

13 Parsnips are shaped like carrots and have a potatolike flavor.

14 Chinese cabbage is grown in stalks and should be heavy and undamaged.

15 Red Swiss chard has large leaves with heavy red or yellow veins.

16 Spaghetti squash should be heavy with a rind that yields to gentle pressure.

17 Yellow chili peppers are hot peppers that should be well-shaped and firm. Avoid any with soft spots or wrinkled skin.

18 Gingerroot, although a seasoning, is a gnarled, brown root found in the produce section.

19 Nopals are leaves of a cactus, eaten as a vegetable. They taste like green beans but are firmer.

20 Chayote are edible gourds with a delicate flavor similar to squash.

21 Zucchini is another summer squash whose dark green rind should yield to gentle pressure.

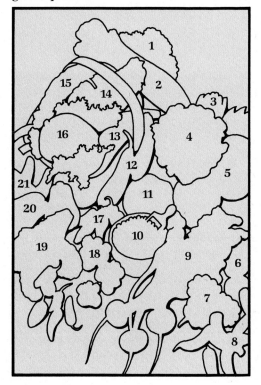

SALADS · SANDWICHES

CHEF'S CASHEW SALAD

Provides 32% U.S. RDA of protein per serving—

- 4 cups torn iceberg lettuce
- 4 cups torn romaine
- 2 medium tomatoes, cut into wedges
- 1 cup shredded mozzarella cheese
- ½ cup sliced turnip
- ½ cup cashews
- 2 hard-cooked eggs, chilled and sliced
- ½ cup shelled sunflower seed
- ⅔ cup bottled Italian salad dressing

In a bowl combine lettuce, romaine, tomato wedges, mozzarella cheese, turnip slices, cashews, and egg slices. Top with sunflower seed. Pour bottled dressing over salad; toss to coat. Serves 4.

SPINACH FRUIT SALAD

Provides 30% U.S. RDA of protein per serving—

- 1 8-ounce can pineapple chunks (juice pack)
- 4 cups torn fresh spinach
- 1 11-ounce can mandarin orange sections, drained
- 2 kiwi fruits, peeled and sliced
- 4 ounces Gouda cheese, cut into julienne strips
- ¾ cup slivered almonds, toasted
- 1 8-ounce carton orange yogurt
- ¼ cup slivered almonds, toasted

Drain pineapple, reserving ¼ cup juice. Combine pineapple and next 5 ingredients. For dressing, combine reserved pineapple juice and yogurt. Pour over salad; toss to coat. Top with ¼ cup almonds. Makes 4 servings.

LAYERED GARDEN SALAD

Provides 30% U.S. RDA of protein per serving—

- 4 cups torn fresh spinach
- 1 cup shredded Swiss cheese
- 1 10-ounce package (2 cups) frozen peas, thawed
- ½ cup pumpkin seed, toasted
- ¼ cup sliced radishes
- 2 hard-cooked eggs, sliced
- 1½ cups cauliflower flowerets
- ½ cup shredded carrot
- 4 cups torn iceberg lettuce
- ½ cup mayonnaise *or* salad dressing
- 1 3-ounce package cream cheese, softened
- 1 tablespoon milk
- 1 tablespoon lemon juice
- ½ teaspoon salt
- ¼ teaspoon garlic powder
  Dash bottled hot pepper sauce
- ¼ cup shredded Swiss cheese
- 2 tablespoons pumpkin seed, toasted
  Cherry tomatoes, halved (optional)

Place spinach in the bottom of a large glass bowl. Top with the 1 cup shredded cheese, 1¼ *cups* of the peas, the ½ cup pumpkin seed, radishes, egg slices, cauliflower, carrot, and lettuce. In a blender container combine the remaining ¾ cup peas with the mayonnaise; add the next 6 ingredients. Cover; blend till smooth. Spread mixture over top of salad. Cover and chill in the refrigerator several hours. Top with remaining ¼ cup cheese and 2 tablespoons pumpkin seed. If desired, garnish with cherry tomato halves. Toss to coat the vegetables before serving. Serves 6.

84

BARLEY-POTATO SALAD

Provides 28% U.S. RDA of protein per serving—

- ¾ **cup quick-cooking barley**
- 3 **medium potatoes, cooked, peeled, and cubed**
- 1 **cup shredded cheddar cheese**
- ¾ **cup sliced celery**
- ¼ **cup chopped green pepper**
- 2 **hard-cooked eggs, sliced**
- 2 **tablespoons sliced green onion**
- 2 **tablespoons chopped pimiento**
- 1 **8-ounce carton plain yogurt**
- ⅓ **cup mayonnaise *or* salad dressing**
- 1 **tablespoon sugar**
- ½ **teaspoon dry mustard**
  Lettuce leaves
- 1 **tablespoon toasted wheat germ**
- 1 **tablespoon snipped parsley**

Cook barley according to package directions; drain. In a bowl combine barley and potatoes. Sprinkle with a little salt. Add cheese, celery, green pepper, egg slices, green onion, and pimiento; toss lightly. Combine yogurt, mayonnaise, sugar, dry mustard, and ½ teaspoon *salt*. Add to potato mixture; toss to coat. Chill. Serve on lettuce-lined plates. Sprinkle with wheat germ and parsley. Serves 4.

ZUCCHINI TWIST SALAD

Provides 29% U.S. RDA of protein per serving—

- 2 **cups corkscrew macaroni**
- 1 **cup sliced fresh mushrooms**
- 1 **medium zucchini, sliced**
- 1 **cup cubed cheddar cheese**
- ¼ **cup pimiento-stuffed olives**
- 1 **cup mayonnaise *or* salad dressing**
- ¼ **cup chili sauce**
- 2 **hard-cooked eggs, chopped**
- ¼ **cup chopped green pepper**
- 4 **lettuce cups**

Cook macaroni, uncovered, in 2 quarts boiling salted water for 4 minutes. Add mushrooms and zucchini; cook 5 minutes more or till macaroni is tender. Drain; rinse in cold water and drain well. Add cheese. Slice olives. For dressing, combine olives, next 4 ingredients, and dash *salt*. Add to macaroni mixture; cover and chill. Serve in lettuce cups. Serves 4.

HEARTY PASTA SALAD

Provides 33% U.S. RDA of protein per serving—

- 1 **6-ounce Edam cheese**
- 1½ **cups shredded Swiss cheese**
- ⅔ **cup broken walnuts**
- ⅓ **cup dairy sour cream**
- ⅓ **cup mayonnaise *or* salad dressing**
- ¼ **cup sweet pickle relish**
- ¼ **cup chopped green pepper**
- ¼ **cup thinly sliced carrots**
- ¼ **cup sliced green onion**
  Dash salt
  Dash bottled hot pepper sauce
- ¼ **cup chopped, cooked spinach**
- 1 **beaten egg**
- 2 **tablespoons grated Parmesan *or* Romano cheese**
- 2 **tablespoons milk**
- 1 **to 1¼ cups all-purpose flour**
  Lettuce leaves

Cut Edam cheese into ½-inch cubes. Combine with next 10 ingredients. Chill in refrigerator for 2 to 3 hours. Drain spinach. For noodles, combine egg, Parmesan or Romano cheese, milk, spinach, and ½ teaspoon *salt*. Stir in enough of the flour to make a stiff dough. Cover for 10 minutes. On a floured surface roll dough into a 20x16-inch rectangle. Let stand, uncovered, 20 minutes; cut into desired lengths. Spread out and let dry on a rack at least 2 hours. Drop noodles into a large amount of boiling salted water. Cook, uncovered, 10 to 12 minutes or till tender; cool in ice water and drain. Combine noodles with cheese mixture. Serve on lettuce-lined plates. Makes 6 servings.

86

TABOULI-PEA SALAD

Provides 28% U.S. RDA of protein per serving—

- 1 cup bulgur wheat
- 1 10-ounce package frozen peas, thawed
- 4 ounces crumbled feta cheese
- 3 ounces Swiss *or* brick cheese, cut into julienne strips
- ¼ cup olive oil *or* salad oil
- 2 tablespoons lemon juice
- ½ teaspoon dried dillweed
- 1 medium tomato, thinly sliced
  Lettuce leaves

In a bowl combine bulgur and 2 cups *warm water;* let stand 1 hour. Drain well; press out excess water. Stir in peas and cheeses. Combine oil, lemon juice, dillweed, and ¼ teaspoon *salt;* gently toss with bulgur mixture. Arrange tomato slices atop lettuce-lined plates; top with bulgur mixture. Makes 4 servings.

TOFU FRUIT SALAD

Pictured on pages 30 and 31
Provides 29% U.S. RDA of protein per serving—

- 1 pound fresh tofu (bean curd)
- ½ cup orange yogurt
- ¼ cup mayonnaise *or* salad dressing
- 1 teaspoon curry powder
- 4 medium nectarines, sliced
- 1 cup bias-sliced celery
  Lettuce leaves
- ¾ cup peanuts

Drain tofu (see following recipe) and cut into ½-inch cubes. For dressing, in a bowl combine yogurt, mayonnaise or salad dressing, and curry powder. Cover and chill in refrigerator for several hours. Meanwhile, arrange cubed tofu, nectarine slices, and celery on lettuce-lined plates. Spoon dressing over each salad. Top each salad with *3 tablespoons* of peanuts. Makes 4 servings.

WON TON-TOFU SALAD

Provides 28% U.S. RDA of protein per serving—

- 1 pound fresh tofu (bean curd)
- ¼ cup salad oil
- ¼ cup vinegar
- 2 tablespoons sugar
- 1 tablespoon sesame oil *or* salad oil
- 1 teaspoon sesame seed, toasted
- 1 teaspoon salt
- ¼ teaspoon ground ginger
- ¼ teaspoon pepper
- 10 won ton skins (3-inch squares) *or* ½ cup chow mein noodles
  Cooking oil for shallow-fat frying
- 6 cups torn salad greens
- 1 11-ounce can mandarin orange sections, drained
- 1 medium green pepper, cut into ½-inch squares
- 1 cup fresh bean sprouts
- 1 cup cashews

To drain tofu, wrap in a double thickness of cheesecloth or paper toweling. Press gently to extract as much moisture as possible. Cut into ½-inch cubes.

For dressing, in a screw-top jar combine the ¼ cup salad oil, vinegar, sugar, sesame or salad oil, toasted sesame seed, salt, ginger, and pepper. Cover and shake well. Chill in refrigerator.

Cut won ton skins into ¼-inch-wide strips; fry, a few at a time, in shallow hot fat ½ to 1 minute or till crisp and golden, stirring occasionally. Drain well on paper toweling. (Omit frying, if using chow mein noodles.)

Line a large salad bowl with torn salad greens. Top with cubed tofu, mandarin oranges, green pepper, bean sprouts, cashews, and fried won ton skins or chow mein noodles. Shake dressing; pour some over salad and toss. Pass the remaining dressing. Makes 4 servings.

GREENS

Boston Lettuce

Curly Endive

Escarole

Iceberg Lettuce

Leaf Lettuce

Romaine

Spinach

Watercress

Lettuces and greens are salad-making staples. No matter what type of salad greens you buy, they should look fresh and perky. All greens should be stored in the refrigerator in a plastic bag or crisper container. Iceberg and romaine will stay fresh and crisp up to a week when properly stored, but the other varieties tend to droop within a few days.

Several hours before using any greens, remove them from the refrigerator and wash them well under cold running water. Shake off any excess water and pat the greens dry with a kitchen towel or paper toweling. Then return them to the refrigerator. This procedure gives the greens time to become crisp.

To prevent the edges of the greens from becoming brown, tear (never cut) the greens into bite-size pieces. The sole exception to this rule is when you want to serve iceberg lettuce as wedges.

Boston lettuce, along with Bibb lettuce, is a member of the butterhead family of greens. Butterhead greens have soft, pliable leaves with a waxy texture and appearance. They are not crisp or solid.

Curly endive is a member of the endive family of greens. It has frilly, narrow leaves and comes in a large clump that looks like a small bush or shrub.

Escarole is a less-frilly type of endive. It has broad, flat, slightly curled leaves and also grows in a clump that looks like a small bush. Its flavor is mild to slightly bitter.

Iceberg lettuce is the most common type of lettuce and is frequently referred to as "head lettuce." Its crisp, solid leaves are medium green on the outside of the head and pale green to white on the inside. A head of iceberg lettuce is firm enough to easily slice into wedges. If you plan to use iceberg lettuce within a week, firmly strike the core of the head against a flat surface to remove it. Use your fingers to lift and twist out the core. Hold the head under cold running water to wash and separate the leaves, then turn the head of lettuce core side down to drain. Store the lettuce in the refrigerator.

Leaf lettuce encompasses many varieties that may be red or green. The one distinguishing characteristic of all leaf lettuce is that it grows as single leaves. Leaf lettuce tends to be tender and sometimes slightly bitter.

Romaine is an elongated leaf of lettuce with coarse, crisp, dark green leaves. Romaine tends to have a stronger flavor than other greens.

Spinach is well-known as a cooked vegetable, but it is also tasty as a raw vegetable. The heavy center vein in spinach leaves should be removed before the spinach is torn into bite-size pieces.

Watercress has a moderately pungent flavor and makes a good addition to a salad. Its leaves are delicate and frilly.

88

SPROUT SALAD

Provides 29% U.S. RDA of protein per serving—

 2 cups fresh bean sprouts
 2 cups fresh alfalfa sprouts
 ¾ cup broken pecans
 ½ cup thinly bias-sliced carrot
 ½ cup coarsely chopped cucumber
 ½ cup pitted whole dates, snipped
 1 8-ounce carton plain yogurt
 ½ teaspoon sugar
 ¼ teaspoon ground cinnamon
 2 tablespoons sesame seed, toasted

Combine first 3 ingredients; toss. Place on 2 serving plates. Arrange carrot, cucumber, and dates atop. For dressing, combine yogurt, sugar, and cinnamon; pour over the salads. Top with sesame seed. Makes 2 servings.

DELUXE DINNER SALAD

Provides 33% U.S. RDA of protein per serving—

 1 15-ounce can garbanzo beans
 4 cups torn iceberg lettuce
 2 medium tomatoes, cut into wedges
 1 cup sliced cauliflower flowerets
 1 cup thinly sliced carrots
 1 small cucumber, sliced
 4 hard-cooked eggs, sliced
 ½ small onion, thinly sliced and
     separated into rings
 1 small cucumber, finely chopped
 1 8-ounce carton plain yogurt
 ¼ cup milk
 1 tablespoon sugar
 ¼ teaspoon garlic salt
 1 tablespoon sesame seed, toasted

Drain beans. Place lettuce on 4 serving plates; top with beans, tomato, cauliflower, carrot, cucumber, egg, and onion; chill in refrigerator. To make dressing, combine the remaining ingredients *except* sesame seed; pour over the salads. Top with sesame seed. Makes 4 servings.

BEAN AND CHEESE SANDWICHES

Provides 31% U.S. RDA of protein per serving—

 1 8-ounce can red kidney beans
 1 5-ounce jar American cheese
     spread
 ½ cup shredded Swiss cheese
 1 tablespoon milk
 ⅛ teaspoon garlic powder
 ¼ cup broken walnuts
 2 tablespoons snipped parsley
 4 English muffins, split
     Butter *or* margarine

Drain beans. Stir together cheese spread and next 3 ingredients. Gently stir in kidney beans, walnuts, and parsley. Spread *each* English muffin half with butter and cheese mixture. Broil 4 inches from heat 3 to 5 minutes or till hot. Serves 4.

APPLE-CHEESE MUFFINS

Pictured on pages 31 and 32
Provides 33% U.S. RDA of protein per serving—

 1 cup cream-style cottage cheese
 1 3-ounce package cream cheese,
     softened
 1 medium apple, cored and halved
     crosswise
 ½ cup shredded cheddar cheese
 ⅓ cup shelled sunflower seed
 4 English muffins, split, toasted, and
     buttered
 1 cup fresh alfalfa sprouts

In a mixer bowl combine cottage cheese and cream cheese; beat at low speed of electric mixer till blended. Beat at high speed till fluffy. Chop *half* of the apple; stir into cheese mixture. Stir in cheddar cheese and sunflower seed. Slice the remaining apple half; arrange on muffin halves. Spread with cheese mixture; top with alfalfa sprouts. Makes 4 servings.

HOT EGGS AND CHEESE SANDWICH LOAVES

Provides 33% U.S. RDA of protein per serving—

4 **individual French rolls**
½ **cup dairy sour cream**
1 **slightly beaten egg**
¼ **teaspoon ground coriander**
¼ **teaspoon pepper**
⅛ **teaspoon salt**
   Dash garlic powder
     • • •
3 **hard-cooked eggs, chopped**
½ **cup shredded cheddar cheese
   (2 ounces)**
½ **cup finely chopped celery**
¼ **cup finely chopped green pepper**
¼ **cup sliced pimiento-stuffed olives**
2 **slices provolone cheese, cut in
   half (2 ounces)**
1 **tablespoon butter *or* margarine,
   melted**

Cut a ½-inch lengthwise slice off the top of *each* individual French roll. Scoop out the center of the roll, leaving a shell about ½ inch thick. Reserve the center bread pieces; crumble pieces and measure 1 cup bread crumbs.

In a mixing bowl combine sour cream, the slightly beaten egg, ground coriander, pepper, salt, and garlic powder. Stir in the chopped eggs, shredded cheddar cheese, chopped celery, chopped green pepper, and sliced olives. Stir in the 1 cup reserved bread crumbs.

Fill *each* roll with ¼ *cup* of the egg mixture. Top *each* with ½ slice of provolone cheese. Spread remaining egg mixture atop cheese. Replace the roll tops. Brush with melted butter or margarine.

Place filled rolls on a baking sheet; cover loosely with foil. Bake in a 400° oven about 30 minutes or till filling mixture is heated through. Serve filled rolls while hot. Makes 4 servings.

CAMEMBERT-APRICOT-FILLED PITAS

Provides 36% U.S. RDA of protein per serving—

1 **8¾-ounce can unpeeled apricot
   halves, drained and chopped**
1 **4-ounce package Camembert
   cheese, chilled and cut into
   ½-inch cubes**
⅔ **cup slivered almonds, toasted**
½ **cup lemon yogurt**
1 **pita bread round
   Lettuce leaves**
½ **cup fresh alfalfa sprouts**

Combine apricots, cheese, almonds, and yogurt. Mix well. Halve pita bread crosswise; line inside with lettuce leaves. Spoon cheese mixture into lettuce-lined bread. Top with sprouts. Serves 2.

POCKET OF VEGETABLES

Provides 29% U.S. RDA of protein per serving—

½ **cup cream-style cottage cheese**
2 **tablespoons plain yogurt**
¼ **teaspoon dried marjoram,
   crushed**
1 **avocado, seeded and peeled**
1 **cup shredded farmer cheese**
1 **medium tomato, chopped**
½ **cup slivered almonds, toasted**
2 **pita bread rounds
   Lettuce leaves**
½ **cup fresh alfalfa sprouts**

In a blender container combine cottage cheese, yogurt, marjoram, and ¼ teaspoon *salt*. Cover; blend till smooth. Chop avocado. Combine avocado, cheese, tomato, and almonds. Season with salt and pepper to taste. Halve pita bread crosswise; line inside with lettuce leaves. Fill with vegetable mixture. Top *each* with a dollop of the cottage cheese mixture, then with sprouts. Makes 4 servings.

Pocket of Vegetables

BULGUR SALAD POCKETS

Provides 26% U.S. RDA of protein per serving—

- **1 8-ounce can pineapple chunks (juice pack)**
- **1 tablespoon instant beef bouillon granules**
- **¾ cup bulgur wheat**
- **½ cup raisins**
- **½ cup toasted wheat germ**
- **½ cup sliced celery**
- **¼ cup shredded carrot**
- **½ cup plain yogurt**
- **3 tablespoons mayonnaise**
- **¼ teaspoon dried tarragon, crushed**
- **2 pita bread rounds**
  Cashew Nut Butter (see tip)
  Lettuce leaves

Drain pineapple, reserving juice. Add bouillon and *water* to make 1½ cups liquid. Heat just till warm. Pour over bulgur and raisins; let stand for 1 hour. Drain well. Combine pineapple, bulgur mixture, wheat germ, celery, and carrot. Combine yogurt, mayonnaise, and tarragon; stir into bulgur mixture. Halve bread rounds crosswise. Spread inside with Cashew Nut Butter; line with lettuce. Spoon ¼ of bulgur mixture into each. Serves 4.

Tip: It's easy to make Cashew Nut, Peanut, or Sesame Seed Butter. Just place a steel blade in a food processor work bowl and add 1 cup nuts or seeds. Process 5 to 7 minutes or till butter reaches the desired smoothness, stopping often to scrape sides of bowl. Cover and chill any leftover butter. Note: If using a blender, add nuts; cover and blend.

PEANUT BUTTER AND YOGURT SANDWICH

Provides 28% U.S. RDA of protein per serving—

- **½ cup chopped celery**
- **⅓ cup orange yogurt**
- **⅓ cup Peanut Butter (see tip)**
- **¼ cup chopped raisins**
- **4 slices whole wheat bread**

Stir together first 4 ingredients; spread mixture on bread slices. If desired, top 2 slices with lettuce leaves or alfalfa sprouts. Place remaining slices atop with filling to the inside. Serves 2.

TAHINI-BEAN BOATS

Provides 38% U.S. RDA of protein per serving—

- **1 15-ounce can garbanzo beans**
- **3 tablespoons lemon juice**
- **¼ cup chopped onion**
- **1 clove garlic, minced**
- **2 teaspoons cooking oil**
- **½ cup sesame seed, toasted**
- **¼ cup Sesame Seed Butter (see tip)**
- **¼ cup chopped green pepper**
- **2 pita bread rounds**
- **1½ cups shredded lettuce**
- **1½ cups crumbled feta cheese**
- **1 medium tomato, chopped**
- **⅓ cup sliced ripe olives**

Drain garbanzo beans, reserving 3 tablespoons liquid. Place beans, reserved liquid, and lemon juice in a blender container or food processor; cover and blend or process till pureed. Cook onion and garlic in oil till tender. Combine pureed beans, onion mixture, sesame seed, Sesame Butter, and green pepper; mix well. Split pita rounds horizontally; toast in a 350° oven for 5 minutes. Top *each* half with lettuce; add about ½ cup bean mixture. Top with cheese, tomato, and olives. Serves 4.

92

BARBECUED BEAN ROLL-UPS

Provides 38% U.S. RDA of protein per serving —

¾ cup dry pinto beans
3 cups water
½ teaspoon salt
⅓ cup chopped onion
¼ cup bottled barbecue sauce
¼ teaspoon garlic salt
   Cottage Cheese Pastry
1 cup shredded Monterey Jack
   cheese (4 ounces)
½ cup dairy sour cream
8 pitted ripe olives

Rinse pinto beans. In a saucepan combine pinto beans and water; bring to boiling. Simmer, uncovered, for 2 minutes. Remove from heat. Cover; let stand 1 hour. *Do not* drain. Add salt. Bring to boiling. Reduce heat; simmer, covered, 1 hour or till tender. Drain beans and mash slightly. Stir in chopped onion, bottled barbecue sauce, and garlic salt.

Make the Cottage Cheese Pastry. On a floured surface roll pastry into a 16x12-inch rectangle.

Spread bean mixture over dough; sprinkle with shredded Monterey Jack cheese. Roll up jelly roll style, beginning from longest side. Moisten and seal seam. Cut crosswise into 8 slices; place seam side down in a greased 12x7½x2-inch baking dish. Bake in a 375° oven about 25 minutes or till light brown. Top *each* roll with *1 tablespoon* of the sour cream and a ripe olive. Makes 4 servings.

Cottage Cheese Pastry: Stir together 1 cup all-purpose *flour,* 2 teaspoons *baking powder,* 1 teaspoon *sugar,* ¼ teaspoon *salt,* and ¼ teaspoon *cream of tartar.* Cut in ⅓ cup *shortening* till pieces are the size of small peas. Add ⅔ cup sieved cream-style *cottage cheese.* Toss with a fork till moistened. Form into a ball.

SPANISH RICE ROLLS

Provides 38% U.S. RDA of protein per serving —

¼ cup sliced celery
¼ cup chopped onion
2 tablespoons chopped green
   pepper
1 tablespoon cooking oil
1 7½-ounce can tomatoes
¾ cup water
½ cup brown rice
¼ cup chili sauce
½ teaspoon Worcestershire sauce
¼ teaspoon salt
⅛ teaspoon pepper
   Dash bottled hot pepper
   sauce
      • • •
1 cup shredded Monterey Jack *or*
   cheddar cheese
¾ cup pumpkin seed, toasted
4 individual French rolls
   Lettuce leaves
½ cup dairy sour cream

In a skillet cook sliced celery, chopped onion, and chopped green pepper in cooking oil till vegetables are tender. Stir in *undrained* tomatoes, water, *uncooked* brown rice, chili sauce, Worcestershire sauce, salt, pepper, and bottled hot pepper sauce.

Bring to boiling; reduce heat. Cover and simmer for 1 hour or till liquid is absorbed and brown rice is tender. Remove from heat. Stir shredded Monterey Jack or cheddar cheese and toasted pumpkin seed into brown rice mixture.

Cut a ½-inch lengthwise slice off the top of *each* French roll; scoop out the centers of each roll, leaving a shell about ½ inch thick. Line the inside of each individual French roll with lettuce leaves.

Spoon the rice-cheese mixture atop lettuce. Top each roll with a dollop of sour cream. Replace each of the French roll tops. Makes 4 servings.

INDEX

D–H

L–M